RECALCULATING

Find Financial Success and Never Feel Lost Again

Darren Coleman, PFP, CFP, FCSI

Norsemen Books

Norseman Books is a registered trademark.

Coleman, Darren L., 1969-

Also issued in electronic format

ISBN

Paperback: 978-1-988172-15-6

eBook: 978-1-988172-16-3

1. Financial Planning. 2. Investing. 3. Wealth Management

Printed and bound in the U.S.A.

Published by Norseman Books

Edited by Boni Wagner-Stafford of BClear Writing

www.recalculatingwealth.com

*ATTENTION CORPORATIONS, UNIVERSITIES, COLLEGES AND PROFESSIONAL ORGANIZATIONS: Quantity discounts are available on bulk purchases of this book for educational or gift purposes, or for premiums for increasing memberships. Special book covers or book excerpts can be created to fit specific needs. For more information, please contact Norsemen Books: info@norsmenbooks.com or 1-207-734-4950.

Table of Contents

Prologue

We're lost.

I'm driving through a snowstorm near Collingwood, Ontario with Susan, the woman who would become my wife. I have no idea which way we're supposed to go. It's 1992 and there's no GPS, no Waze and no Google Maps. I do have a cell phone, though. It came with the car. Unfortunately, Cantel's airtime charges are so high I'm afraid to use it. And who am I going to call, anyway? I can't let anyone know I'm lost!

We come across a lonely gas station, sitting at a crossroads marked by four-way stop signs. Sue tells me to go in and ask for directions. We argue. She does not understand that asking for directions is one of the most testosterone-reducing actions an adult male can undertake. The snow is blowing, so I relent. But I use the excuse that we should top up the gas tank first. I'll pay inside and if I happen to ask for some general assistance from the clerk with respect to location, then I can maintain some pride.

So I do. I'm not sure if you've ever had the experience of asking for directions in a small town, but the clerk gave them to me as though I also lived there. Her answer to my query went something like this:

"Oh, you're pretty close to 26. All you have to do is keep going this way, down past the Campbell's place, you know, just past where they were going to put in the drive-in and then look for the garage with the guy who fixes Corvettes. I think it's got a red roof, of course you can't tell right now cause there's a foot of snow on it. Anyway, turn left there and keep going until you see the teacher's place. She's the one who sells pottery in the summer. Then you'll be close."

I thanked her, paid for the gas, opened the door, heard the chime of the bell above my head and marched through the blowing snow back to the car.

When I got in, Sue asked me, "So - what did they say? How do we get there?"

I said, "She told me to turn right."

Introduction

I think GPS is one of man's great inventions. And it was invented by man, not by woman, as only a man would consider spending billions of dollars and launching a network of satellites into space just to avoid admitting he's lost and asking for directions.

I've heard that panic is the mother of invention. If you've ever been at a friend's house for a dinner party and had the toilet water start moving back up on you, then you know exactly what I mean. That's how many men feel when they're lost. That's definitely how men feel when they have to ask for directions. They would rather blindly soldier on. And then discover things like new continents. Magellan, Marco Polo, Christopher Columbus, Francis Drake – all were lost and refused to quit.

Enter GPS

Global Positioning System (GPS) is a navigation system that uses satellites to provide location and time information in all weather conditions anywhere on Earth. The system, initially developed in the early 1970's, operated with only twenty-four satellites.

While originally intended only for military use, it was a civilian tragedy that prompted the United States to make GPS available for commercial and personal use.

On September 1, 1983 Korean Airlines flight KAL007, departing from Anchorage, Alaska on its way to Seoul, Korea strayed off course and into USSR airspace. The airliner was shot down by a Soviet SU-15 jet fighter. All passengers and crew on board – 269 innocent souls – were killed.

Two weeks after the tragedy, President Reagan proposed to make GPS available to avoid navigational error from ever again leading to such a catastrophe. While by no means the only reason, the Korean Airlines disaster was a major catalyst toward civilian access to GPS. Which happened in 1995.

Men the world over have been saying 'thank you' ever since.

How Does GPS Help Us Now?

One of the most remarkable capabilities of GPS now is that it is easily possible to carry the entire road system of the world on one small, portable, battery-operated unit.

Many cars come equipped with satellite navigation systems built into their dashboards. And today almost every smartphone contains a full featured GPS system and mapping application. No need for an additional appliance.

The key features of a modern GPS device are:

- Current location
- Desired location or destination
- Route options
- Points of interest or waypoints
- Traffic conditions

In "*Recalculating: Find Financial Success and Never Feel Lost Again*" I will discuss each of these features in turn and how they can help you in mapping your financial journey as effectively as your road trips.

I will also talk about at how you might handle other problems on the road and how to get to your destination most effectively.

While not always true, many men feel that asking for directions means owning up to a mistake. For them it is an admission that they missed something, that they screwed up. Asking for help may trigger fear they'll lose some independence of spirit.

Consider what happens if you miss a turn, get off on the wrong exit or get lost. Not only do you have to figure out what went wrong, you need to plot a course back to where you should be.

Here's where the wonder and power of the GPS comes in.

Consider that you can now purchase a device, often for as little as $100, that connects you with a network of satellites that can locate your position anywhere on the planet. Furthermore, that little device can navigate to almost anywhere else in the world through an incredible maze of highways, roadways and laneways and give you vital information such as speed limits, on and off ramps, toll roads and key points of interest. Most of them can also provide a choice of routes (fastest, shortest, most economical, for example) and some will even provide current traffic conditions. And all of them will give an estimate of distance and arrival time.

You are now free to travel anywhere, anytime, and are forever freed from having to ask for directions. If you've used a GPS device, you know how incredibly liberating it is to navigate to almost any destination with complete independence, freedom and confidence. You now have the luxury to go where you want without being concerned about how to get there.

You also have the flexibility to change your plans on a whim. And if you miss an exit or turn left instead of right, it doesn't scold. There is no argument. It simply says, "recalculating". The GPS gets busy finding a new way to get where you want to go. And if your destination changes, or you need to make a detour, the GPS unit will do that work too. You have the tools to make the car go where you want, when you want, with greater safety and comfort than ever before.

You are never lost.

You also have the ability to try new routes with only a little bit of bravery. Going not just where the road is supposed to lead but trying something new with the full confidence that the satellites and GPS device will guide you back on-route whenever you choose. Because it will never lose sight of you and it always knows the way.

People have the same issues with money as they do with navigating while driving. After nearly twenty-five years as a professional financial advisor and certified financial planner, I regularly encounter people who are not where they thought they would be. Indeed, that's why they come and see me. Some are off course and not sure how to get back.

Today, are you where you thought you'd be fifteen years ago? In other words, fifteen years ago (or ten or twenty – it's your game, so play it how you want) when you thought about your future, what did you see? Are you where you imagined you would be? Have things turned out as you intended?

You might not be in the financial position you had hoped. Something has happened so that you are off course. Maybe your work wasn't as successful as you wanted it to be. Maybe you had a personal, health or other financial challenge that you had to deal with. Perhaps you had to help someone else in their journey. For whatever reason, you feel a bit lost and want to find a way to get back on track.

Or maybe you are ahead of where you expected. Fate has smiled on you and you've reached your destination. You've reached the goals you had for yourself but you don't think you are done yet. Now, the challenge is to answer, "What's next?"

It could also be that you've been so busy living your life day-to-day, that you have simply wound up where you are. And you're not sure where that is exactly. And you're not sure where you'd really like to go.

I have also seen many situations where couples are realizing that each partner wants to go to a different place. This often happens right at retirement, when the forty to sixty hours a week that people spent away from their spouses at work suddenly disappears. Some relationships are unable to withstand such a dramatic change of scenery so quickly. I suspect this is why divorce rates spike within 5 years of retirement[1].

Perhaps you're just starting out. Life is before you and it can either be a daily grind or a wonderful adventure. There are so many choices ahead – and you want to be sure you learn to drive well.

In all of these cases, and many more, the one thing everyone has in common is in wanting help in reaching a destination, in reaching desired outcomes. And no one likes asking for directions.

Throughout this book, I'll make reference to clients I've worked with and situations that I've seen. Names and some circumstances have been changed to protect the confidentiality of each client.

I always say that I only work with nice people. One of the great joys in my profession is *helping great people live their greatest lives.* Sharing their stories to help others is a wonderful privilege.

This book is intended to be like a GPS for your financial journey.

---

[1] Source: Statistics Canada, Marital Status Overview, 2011, Anne Milan, published July 2013

Life is a series of choices: some conscious, many not.

The road is yours, and while there may be rules to follow and you don't get to pick every turn or control the traffic, you do have control over your choice of destination and how you drive.

So, here's to freedom and life on the open road.

1

When Things Go Off Course

"Life is what happens
when you are making other plans."
– John Lennon

Something has gone wrong. You're off course. Maybe you've hit a pot hole or run out of gas. Maybe you had an accident or got lost in a detour. Or you helped someone else and damaged your own car. Whatever the reason, your financial progress has slowed or stopped and you're not moving in the direction you wanted, as quickly as you wanted.

An early warning that you're off course gives you the most time and best chance of correcting any problems.

The first step in solving a problem is actually knowing there is a problem.

The same way a GPS unit tracks your progress and the route you are supposed to be following, alerting you the moment you've missed a turn, you need a system that can monitor data and trigger the same alert on your financial journey. You need a financial dashboard to check your status: am I on course?

If your plan called for you to be debt-free in four years, are you halfway there after two? If you expected to have $500,000 in your RRSP by age forty-five, do your statements show that balance by your forty-fifth birthday?

A sailor will take a compass bearing to calculate his exact position. A driver will check her dashboard and gauges. You need to do a quick financial check and run some numbers.

- What's my net worth right now?

- How much did I save this year?

- Does my budget reflect the reality of my lifestyle, and do I need some behaviour modifications?

- How has my portfolio performed in the past few months?

- Am I where I was supposed to be?

Check the Dashboard

While there are an infinite number of reasons you may be off course, in my experience most of those reasons relate to the same conditions.

Out of Gas

Failing to save enough money is the primary reason for not being where you thought you would be by now. Determining how much you need to save to reach your waypoints and destinations and milestones is the first step in planning.

Easy to say: much harder to do. It's like losing weight. All you have to do is eat less and exercise more. Right? Not quite as simple as it sounds.

The trick is in having the discipline to make the savings happen.

Your behaviour must align with your goals.

If you're finding that it doesn't, then perhaps you're not being honest with yourself about what it is you really do want. This isn't usually a math problem – it's a behavioural one.

In chapter four, *Habits for a Successful Trip*, I will outline the best ways to keep you on track with your savings goals.

Making saving a priority is a challenge at least in part due to the messages from mass media. Media and popular entertainment have given us a very screwed up version of reality. For example, nearly every television sitcom shows people living a lifestyle that their fictional occupation would not allow them to afford. I still cannot figure out how the chronically underemployed twenty-somethings on Friends paid for those apartments in Manhattan. People Magazine found that, in 2014, a two-bedroom, one-bath apartment in the West Village would rent for $5,100/month. There's no way that Monica and Rachel could have afforded their place, even if it was an illegal sublet from Monica's grandmother.

So, first things first. Stop trying to live the lifestyle you see on TV. It's as real as the laugh track.

Flat Tire

It's not uncommon for a market correction to impact your nest egg. Every driver gets a flat tire. Perhaps the tire was worn out. Maybe you picked up a nail. Or you hit a pothole somewhere along the way. Regardless of how it happened, you need to pull over, get the problem fixed and then get back on the road. You don't get out of the car and walk just because you got a flat.

However, when investing, I see people wanting to do this all the time. At a 5 percent correction, they think the car has broken down. At a 10 percent correction, they want to get out of the car and take the bus. At a 20 percent correction, life as they know it is over and they think they've driven off the cliff like Thelma and Louise. All of these emotional responses are understandable. And all of them are dangerous.

I recently met with a potential client who said her previous investment manager lost her over one hundred thousand dollars.

I asked, "How did that happen? Was it a bad investment?"

No, she said. She went against his advice in 2009 and sold everything she had right at the bottom of the market.

"I panicked. I thought that I couldn't afford to lose any more money."

Tragically, she created the precise scenario she was afraid of, as almost all the securities she sold had fully rebounded less than eighteen months later. The problem was never her investments; it was what she did with them. By jumping out of the car while it was still moving, she hurt herself to the point where she may never fully recover financially.

Market corrections, like flat tires, are a fact of life.

They are unfortunate, but they do happen. You can't always avoid them, so if you're going to drive, it's best to learn how to navigate around them. And it's critical to know the difference between a tire that needs to be changed from one that just needs more air. If the investment is still solid but just temporarily down, then adding to the position – buying more – when it's cheaper is a winning strategy.

Car Crash

Some crashes happen due to bad driving, either by you or by others. Others are simply a matter of being in the wrong place at the wrong time. Regardless of the cause, you need to assess the damage, make repairs and get moving again.

Financial accidents can take many forms. Perhaps you lost your job. Maybe you or someone in the family got sick and could not work.

If you've driven the car into the ditch, then we can likely tow you out, repair the damage and get you back on your way. To make up for lost time, you might be able to drive better or skip a waypoint. If you've taken on too much debt, for example, then maybe you need a year of austerity (no vacations, no big ticket spending) to get back on track.

If something more severe has happened, like a job loss or an illness, then perhaps you need to revisit some of the critical parts of your plan to be sure you can still make the trip.

Liz's Story

When I met Liz, she was addicted to the Shopping Channel. She was in her late fifties and going deeply into debt. She recently left a well-paying government job and was taking an early retirement pension. Her retirement wasn't planned; it came about due to a disability. Not long after leaving work, she found herself at home, depressed and alone. With little to do, and no one to share her life with, she watched the Shopping Channel for hours on end and began ordering trinkets and trash, literally by the truck load. Her purchases became compulsive and soon she had a garage full of boxes – most of them unopened.

When I began working with Liz, it was to help her manage the pension that she had commuted from her government job. I discovered there was a problem after she began requesting withdrawals that were larger than her plan required, and larger than her plan could support.

The first time she asked for a lump sum, I didn't inquire, because I appreciate that sometimes life happens. When she asked for a second withdrawal eight months later, I asked why. She said she had run up some unexpected debt. She's a grown up, so I let it go. But at the third request less than a year later, I pushed for more of an explanation. I said, "Ok, Liz, you need to come clean with me. What's going on? Why are you off-plan by so much?"

And that's when the dam broke.

She said that watching the Shopping Channel was exciting and the hosts were very engaging. Moreover, she said that phoning in to the show and talking to one of the order-takers made her feel better. She was desperately lonely and her solution to having human contact meant maxing out her credit card and having a garage and basement full of unopened boxes of crap.

As we dug deeper together, it was clear that Liz's financial issue was a symptom of an emotional issue. When she left her job, she lost her network of friends and co-workers. Worse, she felt that no one wanted her and she was worthless. The Shopping Channel gave her positive feelings of empowerment, belonging and companionship.

To really help Liz, I had to address both the financial accident and the emotional wreckage. First, I worked with the Shopping Channel to return several truckloads of unopened merchandise. The refund helped reduce the debt. Second, Liz and I cancelled most of her credit and got her into credit counselling. Third, and perhaps most importantly, she began volunteering through Meals on Wheels, a charity service that delivers affordable meals to help those who are unable to shop or cook for themselves to maintain their independence. Most of their clients are retired people, just like Liz.

After a few months, Liz told me that she felt completely renewed and refreshed. She was now connected to other people who, like her, were also not connected. She had made several new friends, as her appointments were becoming more social calls than food deliveries. She was important, respected and knew that she was needed. She had found a new community and her role within it.

I think I did two critical things in helping Liz. First, I identified the problem and took action to fix it, both financially and emotionally. Second, I never blamed her for having her problems. It was a situation that had a cause and an effect. She wasn't a bad person. She was a good person having a bad time. And I believe that when I showed respect for her, acknowledging and respecting her inherent value, Liz trusted me enough to be open to my help.

Detour

Financial detours can either be obstacles or opportunities that take us in an unexpected direction.

In some cases, it could be that employment has changed. You've been downsized, dismissed or your job has changed.

In other cases, a financial opportunity may arise that you must take advantage of. My brother relocated from Toronto to Boston to take a better job and has built a life in the U.S.A. We've had many clients buy companies, buy properties and take on new opportunities simply because it made sense to do so.

Being both financially able and emotionally ready to respond and react is the key to making detours successful. The detour may be longer than the original route, so it's important to have enough gas in the car at all times. You also have to make a decision: will you take a different route to your goal, or map out a new destination?

Help A Stranded Motorist

Not every problem is yours. And you're not on this journey alone. Sometimes you need to stop and help someone else who has had a problem. These are often hitchhikers you had to pick up. I'm talking about people close to you who need help. They've run out of gas, had a fender bender, locked their keys in the car or found themselves in a ditch.

When a child, a family member or a best friend needs your help, you simply must find a way to help them. I'm starting to see baby boomers who are discovering their retirement will include their parents' retirement. As Mom and Dad are living meaningfully into their eighties, they will need emotional, physical and perhaps even financial support for many years. Susan Hyatt, CEO and Founder of Silver Sherpa and an expert in smart aging tells me that the primary caregiver for a retired person is the eldest daughter or daughter-in-law. Giving time and money to take care of elderly parents rarely fits into the retirement planning of most fifty-year-olds. But it should, because it probably will.

The housing market, in both Canada and the U.S., has also created many instances where people's financial plans collide. In Canada, as the cost of housing in many urban markets has stretched to the limits of affordability, many parents are helping their twenty-something children come up with a down payment. In the U.S., after the housing bubble burst in 2008-2009, many found they could not keep their homes without some financial support from their parents or siblings.

The first rule when helping others is to make sure you are safe first.

On an airplane, during the safety briefing, the flight attendant tells you to put your own oxygen mask on before helping someone else.

The same rule applies when helping out in someone else's financial accident. Don't hurt yourself in trying to help them. Pull off the roadway and assess the situation. If the problem is beyond your training, resources or ability to fix, then call for help. A fool and a failed hero are the same thing.

Driving Solo

Losing a spouse through death means big changes as you are now forced to drive alone. And it's even more difficult if you don't know how to drive.

A few months ago I met Lydia. She had recently lost her husband, and he was the one who had been looking after all of their financial details. She had no idea how to do the banking or manage the investments. She was completely unaware of their debts and was uncomfortable even going to the bank.

When I began working with her, my first step was to collect all of her documents so together we could see her complete financial situation. She had a substantial line of credit at her bank, and when I reviewed the statement, I noticed a line item for an insurance payment.

It turns out that her late husband had fully insured the debt! She had been making payments on a loan that would disappear as soon as she filed the proper claim forms.

While Lydia and I dealt with the short-term issues, her financial car was effectively parked on the side of the road. Her driver and companion was gone and the plan she had for herself is now permanently changed.

How will she spend the next thirty years? She not only has to put the pieces of her life back together and find a new destination, she also has to learn how to drive.

My role is to teach her and to find the right pacing so that only decisions that have to be made today are made today. I need to help her get the car moving again, stepping in, for now, as her chauffeur while she learns to drive.

Swapping Drivers

Divorce and remarriage also bring new changes that are very similar to those faced when losing a spouse. You suddenly find you are driving solo, you need to learn to drive on your own, just as Lydia did.

But getting a new driver, a new life partner, brings many new issues. First, they may have a different driving style from you. They may drive faster, slower, more aggressively or defensively. Appreciating that they have different attitudes and habits around money is critical. And if they're a bad driver, prone to financial accidents and with a terrible record, then perhaps you don't let them drive.

Second, it could be tricky putting everyone's luggage in the same trunk. Their financial baggage may be larger and more problematic than yours. Just like packing for a trip, sometimes you need to carefully assess what you can take on the journey. Not everything will fit. And sometimes you need to buy new luggage together.

I see this regularly when two adults try to blend their financial lives. They both come to the new relationship with fully-formed money habits as well as assets, debts and commitments.

An open and honest review of each party's financial position is critical to making the new partnership work. Opening up the fiscal kimono is the true test of a relationship!

In some cases, it's better to take two cars. Each person can then pack their own bags, take what they want, drive the way they want and be responsible for their own maintenance. For many people starting out in a new relationship, this is the smartest course. It may not be as romantic, but it works better.

There's no argument over who pays for gas or what radio station is playing. You manage your own spending, saving and investing and they manage theirs. You can agree to meet at the same waypoints and destinations – you'll just take your own vehicle to get there. When this happens, my role is to coordinate, like a traffic cop, so that each person gets there at the same time.

It's rare that both people will start at the same financial position. Often the person with less money at the start of the relationship may need to drive faster or go without breaks to catch up with their partner in the other car.

Life Happens

Life has movement. Financial markets have movement. Our plans – financial and otherwise – need to have movement.

Things rarely go according to plan. Shit happens. The trick is recognizing that things are a little off course, and then knowing what to do about it.

If, right now, you're not moving as you had hoped to move and your financial position is not what you thought it would be – then you're lost.

The good news is: you can fix it. No problem is too big. And there are only a few key steps to follow to recalculate and get back on track. You must quit making it worse.

Stop the Car

This seems obvious, but it often is not. Stop moving. Stop spending, stop investing, stop taking on new debt and stop ignoring the problem.

To keep moving in the wrong direction will not help. If you're lost, then you'll only get more lost. Hope is not a strategy. The desire to keep going becomes a form of denial.

For example, when I asked Liz why she kept buying things from the Shopping Channel, even when she knew she didn't need more stuff, she said it felt good just to order.

For her, continuing to travel even in the wrong direction felt better than stopping and reflecting on where she was at the moment. She didn't want to discover that she was behaving like a blindfolded passenger and the car was out of control.

So the first step in reclaiming control is to stop the car.

No Blame, No Shame

The next step is perhaps the hardest one to follow because it's not mechanical and it's not mathematical. It's emotional.

Before you can assess your situation, you must defuse it. There is no point in yelling, crying, becoming hostile or defensive. If you're stuck, then shouting will not get you unstuck. It will only slow down the process.

To solve the financial problems, you must park the emotional ones.

Money can mean many things: security, comfort, power, achievement and control.

How you use money is a reflection of how you see and interact with the world. Money is the tool you use to manage life.

Reviewing the seven stages of grief can help guide you through the range of emotions that you, and your passengers, are likely to feel as you move through the Recalculating process.

Shock	What the heck just happened? How'd I lose this money?
Denial	No, no. Everything will be fine. I'll just not open my statements.
Anger	The damn stock market/economy/recession/crisis du jour.
Bargaining	If the stock gets back to what I paid for it, I'm out.
Depression	Investing is too risky. I'm putting everything under the mattress.
Testing	Maybe I'm being too chicken. Things will get better, right?"
Acceptance	OK – I've now got a plan and a professional advisor helping me. Things will be different this time.

Each step of the process takes time to complete, and each person moves through each of the stages at their own speed. Recognizing where you are, and where your family and fellow passengers are, helps tremendously in moving on. Becoming locked into the early stages, particularly denial and anger, is harmful. Indeed, couples can get caught in a feedback loop by blaming each other and never moving past these stages. Perhaps that's why I hear that more than 50 percent of marriages end in divorce, with financial matters being the lead cause.

Getting to the *Testing* and *Acceptance* emotional stages are necessary for the Recalculating process to work. If you're not there yet, then you need to do other work before you get to the math. One technique I've found helpful is to examine the issue as if it were someone else's problem.

Eric and Laura

In 2010, Eric and Laura came to see me. They both had decent jobs, young kids and a desire to retire comfortably. However, they were not on the same page when it came to savings. Eric was very organized and highly focused on achieving his goals. He was willing to defer some luxury today to have security in the future. Laura, on the other hand, wanted to maximize their current lifestyle and enjoy the moment. For her, austerity now means discomfort with no promise that tomorrow will be better.

After hearing what each had to say, I asked them if they could help me with a problem I was trying to solve for another couple. I mentioned that I had met with another family the day before and they were in conflict. I gave them a brief overview of their financial situation, which was remarkably close to their own. The key problem was that the partners did not agree on how to balance their savings and spending. As they were similar in age and place in life, I was curious for Eric and Laura's observations. I asked them: if they were in my shoes as a financial advisor, what advice would they give this couple?

This turned out to be a pivotal moment. Both Eric and Laura were able to see a situation outside of their own and view it from the position of their best selves. The emotion was removed and it became an exercise in problem solving, and not the continuation of an argument. Each gave their perspective and opinion on the best way forward and each had some insight into how the other sees the world.

They realized as we went through the conversation that I had simply reframed their situation and asked them to see it as someone else's problem. This gave them a bird's eye view and kept their emotions in check.

Sometimes when you're up too close you can't see the entire picture. By playing a game of moving it outside of yourself, you can be more objective and find logical, rational solutions. If you're stuck in the blame and shame feedback loop, try viewing the problem as though it were someone else's. What would you advise them to do?

2

Where Am I?

*"If you don't know where you are going,
any road will get you there"*

— *Lewis Carroll*

I n order to plot a new course – one that will get you back on financial track – you need to know where you are right now. A regular examination of your personal net worth statement will keep you in touch with how much you own versus what you owe. It should always be positive! And once positive, it needs to keep growing.

Next, it is important to have a clear understanding of your current cash flow. If you're not saving or you are in debt, then you need to track how money is going through your hands and household.

$ Look at your bank account and credit card statements for the past three months.

$ Organize the items based on your budget.

$ If things are out of whack, then critically examine what spending changes you need to make. Is lifestyle out of control or did a temporary emergency come up? Are there patterns that need to be changed now or was it a one-time issue?

What's My Driving Style?

A key part of your initial assessment is evaluating your emotional connection with money. Just as we drive differently, some slower, some faster, some cautious, some reckless, your experience with money plays a key role in your success.

For many, finding financial success is not a math problem, it is more about behaviour and discipline. For some, it comes from what their parents taught them about money, or what they saw their parents do with money, that provides key insights into how they deal with money.

For example, I have seen situations where mom and dad were very cautious and their children grew up and continued following their example. In other cases, the children felt that their parent's thrift caused them to miss out and so as adults, they are driven to have every luxury in life.

We all have an emotional response to money. Whether you see it as safety, success, power, validation or comfort, it is important to have some appreciation for your basic programming so that you can plan effectively. Only those financial strategies that appeal to and engage your programming will be effective.

So, if you view money as safety, there is a risk that you will invest far too conservatively, as you will focus on risks that are not really there and ignore others that are material.

If you view money as power or status, then you may not be prudent in assessing risk and be overconfident.

If you've always been reckless with money, then I can give you all the best financial techniques out there, but you'll still be reckless with money until you understand why. If you've always hoarded money, then you will continue to hoard money until you understand why.

If you don't know why you do things, then you'll just continue doing what you've always done.

An honest appraisal of your own beliefs, values and preferences about money is critical because you need to know not just where you want to go – you also need to know the style in which you're going to get there. Just like driving: do you like to speed or do you stay in the slow lane?

This assessment takes on another dimension when you consider who is on the journey with you. How does your spouse feel about money? What is their initial programming? In most cases, couples are generally aligned, otherwise they probably would not have decided to be together.

However, it is the emotional response to money that often creates stress fractures in a relationship. While some arguments may be at about the same level as disagreeing over the radio station in the car, others can be very deep and traumatic.

Frank and Priscilla

Let me tell you about clients Frank and Priscilla. Frank inherited a portfolio of blue-chip stocks from his uncle. His uncle had been very careful in investing his money and Frank was impressed by how much the portfolio had grown over time and the dividends he was receiving. So, he was quite surprised when Priscilla told him that her desire was for him to sell the portfolio and pay off their mortgage.

For Priscilla, eliminating the debt and owning their home free and clear was the most sensible strategy. We ran several scenarios for them, showing the mathematical result of each decision – but neither was swayed to change their opinion. Frank wanted to follow in his beloved uncle's footsteps and Priscilla wanted the mortgage gone. There was no agreement or compromise, and the discussion risked becoming heated and emotional as each stuck to their view.

When we dug deeper, we discovered the foundation for each person's decision: For Frank, his uncle was the most financially successful person in his life, and he wanted to emulate him by keeping the portfolio. To him, the money meant permanent security and respect for his uncle's wisdom. Priscilla shared that her father had been a gambler and she grew up with money always being at risk. The mortgage was never paid and they lived in constant fear of financial ruin. To her, the money meant a chance to finally have financial security. And keeping it in stocks was the exact opposite of security. Stocks were risk, and she was not going to have it.

Until we brought these very different belief systems out in the open so that each could hear, understand and respect the other's views, there was no way forward.

With a bit of education on investing and the statistical reality of financial risk, we were able to arrive at a comfortable compromise: 50 percent of the portfolio was to be sold and the mortgage reduced. The balance was to be kept and the dividends reinvested to continue building the portfolio. In this way, Priscilla got a long way towards the financial security she needed, and Frank was able to continue managing his inheritance in the way he wanted. Each person's view and emotional needs were heard and respected.

Current Financial Position

What Do I Own?

Your first step is to look at what you own and distinguish between the ones that are productive and others that are not productive. Some assets will help you on your journey, like gas in the tank. Other assets will help you enjoy life on the road. For example, a ski boat is an asset – but it's not the same as a share of Apple or Royal Bank.

The way you determine the difference is to understand if the item will increase or decrease in value over time.

Some assets, like a gold bar, a share in a great company, or your home are reasonably expected to be worth more over time. So, you should accumulate those as they will help you have a better future.

Let's look at a number of common assets and see where they fit in.

Lifestyle Assets

Many of the things you buy are for comfort and lifestyle. You enjoy them today and understand that they will be worth less as you use them. In short, they depreciate in value over time. These are unproductive assets.

Here are some examples of lifestyle assets:

$ Car

$ Motorcycle

$ Furniture

$ Boat

$ Clothes

$ Electronics

$ Patio furniture, barbecues

$ Laptops, computers, tablets

When I look at most people's initial financial position, it's normal to see lots of unproductive assets and minimal attention paid to accumulating productive assets. I'd say that most people would rather spend more time shopping for a new jacket or TV than on planning their retirement investments.

Along with the fact that these lifestyle assets will be worth less in the future, they are also not marketable while you own them. You can't really sell them to anybody else if you suddenly need to turn the asset into cash.

Here's also where it's important to differentiate between **sellable** and **marketable**. Sellable means you can find a buyer. Marketable means you can sell it at a reasonable price. The item you bought for $10 and sold for fifty cents at a garage sale is sellable. Just because you can sell something, doesn't mean you really should.

While it's easy to sell a share of McDonalds on the stock market (something you can do in less than one second), selling a personal asset means turning to eBay or a yard sale.

When you accumulate assets, it's important to understand precisely what you are accumulating. And spend as much time – or more – paying attention to accumulating those things that will increase your net worth and your lifestyle in the future.

My Home

This one is particularly tricky. Most of us take pride in our homes and often feel they are worth more than the market price indicates. It is entirely normal for real estate agents to find that their clients have a much higher price in mind than they do when they list their properties for sale. Your home is really only worth what someone else will pay for it.

You also have to contend with what I refer to as the siren call of home equity. If you remember Homer's Odyssey from high school, the sirens were dangerous and beautiful creatures who used their enchanting music and voices to lure nearby sailors to shipwreck on the rocky coast.

Home equity can have a similar allure, and this overconfidence in our estimates of its value can also lead us astray and off course.

If you bought your house for $250,000 ten years ago and you hear that your neighbour across the street has listed their home – which is almost identical to yours – for $500,000, what do you instantly think? That your house is worth at least $500,000 too!

And then you start considering all the ways that your home is more valuable: your paint is nicer and your landscaping is a bit better. You have a nicer kitchen or have taken better care of your house. Or maybe they have a fire hydrant and a sidewalk in front, so that must detract from its value and make your house more desirable, right?

Then what do you do? You feel a bit wealthier, don't you? As your home is worth more than you thought, that means *you* are worth more than you thought. So, you're further ahead in your plans so maybe you can spend a bit more this year. You don't need to save as much, because the house is worth more, because the neighbour's house isn't nearly as nice as yours.

And that's when you crash into the rocks that you didn't see.

The big rock beneath the surface was the fact that equity you were counting on is merely an illusion. It's on paper.

It's not real.

> **It can only be real if you sell the house and actually have the money in hand.**

Which you wouldn't really have anyway, as you'd have to take that money and buy another house – which has also gone up in value.

The primary danger of considering home equity as the primary component of your wealth is that you become complacent and stop saving as you should to more liquid and marketable assets.

Indeed, it is very common for me to meet people who are more focused on paying down their mortgage as quickly as possible and saving almost nothing for retirement, their children's education or other goals. In their minds, paying off the house provides the maximum in financial security. It does not.

The second danger is that when people plan for retirement, they include a plan to downsize. This also sounds like a very reasonable plan: sell the house when the kids are gone, buy a smaller property, perhaps in a less expensive part of town and pocket the difference to provide an income. But when it comes time to implement this part of the plan, people are not doing it.

First, the house is not just a roof over their heads and a place to keep their stuff. It's where their families live. It's where they raise their children, help them with homework, hold them when they are sick and celebrate their birthdays. It's where they watch them become the people they love most. It's holidays and arguments. It's where they hold each other when Grandpa dies. It's home – and it's hard to leave. And sometimes the children don't leave.

It is becoming more common for families to have multiple generations living together. Grandparents and grandchildren very often now use the same kitchen. The house is an asset they all share.

In both cases, retirees are staying in their homes longer than they thought and accessing that home equity they were counting on becomes very complicated. They can't sell just their living room.

Even if the house is sold and the downsizing plan is put into place, many find they didn't pocket quite as much as they thought. Realtor's commissions, legal fees, movers and other costs very quickly eat into the surplus they were expecting. And that windfall often tempts instant gratification as major purchases, such as a new car or a Mediterranean cruise, are suddenly possible when there's a lot of cash in the bank. The money that was supposed to last twenty years is quickly gone in five.

Owning a Business

Private businesses are very hard to quantify for a number of reasons.

First, many small businesses have no inventory so there is nothing tangible that we can value. If the company owned property, such as a building and materials, then those will have a value that we can calculate. But if it's a service business, then the value is in what the company can *do*, not what it owns. Businesses that have material inventory, on the other hand, are often worth several times what is in the storeroom.

Second, the real value in the business is its people, their skills and talent. Often, the primary equity is the business owner's technical ability, or their goodwill and the relationships they have. So, if they're not in business anymore, the company cannot survive without them. Few small businesses have value independent of the people who founded and run them. To endure and prosper, the company must develop a structure of processes that are scalable, teachable and repeatable, rather than the embodiment of the owner's personality. When we consider what a business is worth, all of these elements come into play. At the end of the day, a business is only worth what someone else will pay for it.

Rental Properties

A very popular strategy for the past decade has been for investors to buy a number of properties and then rent them out. Along with accumulating real estate assets, the tenants provide a regular stream of rent. This can provide a passive retirement income to the landlord.

In most cases, the investor funds the property purchases with a high degree of debt. So, rather than receiving an income from the properties that they can live on, the rent is used to service the mortgages and maintain the properties. Indeed, many actively use debt to avoid having any net income accrue to them. As long as the costs for keeping the property are more than or equal to the rental income, there may be no current taxes due. The properties run as close to a loss as their accountants will allow.

When I try and calculate the actual value to the investor of these properties, I need to look at the net value: the approximate market value less any mortgages outstanding. I also need to factor in any transaction costs, such as sales commissions and legal fees, plus any capital gains taxes. There's also an item called 'recapture' that applies to any accelerated depreciation that may have been used to defer tax over the years that is repaid upon sale.

I must also try to determine the actual value of keeping the properties as a going concern. What is the true value of the rent? What is the proposed maintenance cost? Future taxes? And being a landlord is not a risk-free venture. Most jurisdictions place very specific legal duties and responsibilities on the landlord that frequently tilt the balance in favour of the tenant. And if you get a bad tenant, they can destroy any economic value you have in the property. They can also cause you headaches in ways you can never imagine and wouldn't wish on your worst enemy.

My client Ruby owned several rental townhouses. She was very comfortable with the strategy and had owned the units for over ten years. Everything was fine and she was looking forward to an enjoyable retirement with her company pension, expecting the properties to contribute at least 50 percent of her desired income.

A great plan – until tenants from hell moved in. They would not allow her access to the property for routine inspections and maintenance for over a year. Then, they stopped paying. After fighting them in court for over six months, the Sheriff finally evicted them. When she was finally able to enter the townhouse, she was heartbroken to discover that there was considerable damage. A leaky pipe in the upstairs washroom went unattended for months and destroyed the kitchen below. The carpets were beyond repair and nearly every wall had to be either fixed or repainted. Her cost, which was unrecoverable from the tenant, was over $100,000. Almost all of her profits from the previous decade were lost – and her retirement would never be what she had hoped.

I told Ruby that she was lucky: at least they hadn't started a marijuana grow-op.

I've seen that situation too. The damage is far more extensive and requires remediation for mold removal that is shockingly expensive. None of which is covered by most home insurance policies because the grow-op is an illegal activity. The damage is then compounded by markedly lower resale value. The unfortunate homeowner is a victim and there is essentially no recourse to the financial damage these criminals cause.

Investments
When you think about investments, you are considering money you have squirreled away for the future. Some people call this savings, others name it after the type of account it's in (RRSP, TFSA, pension plan, etc.).

It's easy to confuse the investment with the box it comes in.

For example, many people think that an RRSP is an investment. It's not. It's simply a special type of account that can hold a wide range of investments.

Tax plays a huge role in investing, with investments often split between those held in tax-assisted plans (called "registered" plans) and those that are not tax-assisted. Tax-assisted plans are like turbocharging your savings and we'll look at those more closely in chapter six, *Getting Underway* when I discuss toll roads and HOV lanes.

What's important first is to appreciate the kinds of investments or asset classes that your accounts can invest in.

Cash & Near-Cash

This is literally money in the bank. It can be in a bank account, a Guaranteed Investment Certificate (GIC) that matures in a year, or a certificate of deposit.

The key elements are that the rate of return is known in advance, and the principal, or original investment, is guaranteed. These investments have essentially no risk to your capital. But they also have almost no return, so they pose tremendous risk to your future.

Fixed Income

These investments are commonly bonds and other vehicles where you are primarily a lender to another party, often a government or a corporation. The terms are longer, a minimum of two years and sometimes stretching to twenty years or more. Your rate of return is higher, and risk comes from the quality of the entity borrowing the money from you. Also, as you have loaned the funds out for a longer period of time, the movement in overall interest rates can also affect your overall return.

Some examples of fixed income investments are:

$ GICs that mature in more than a year

$ Canada Savings Bonds

$ Mortgages

Equity

Equity investments represent ownership, often in a business. Indeed, it has become increasingly easy to become an owner of some of the best companies in the world, either directly by buying their shares, or indirectly by buying a mutual fund or an exchange traded fund, where the shares are acquired on our behalf, and pooling our capital with many other investors.

Equity has a higher degree of capital risk than fixed income because the returns are not known in advance and you stand at the end of the line of creditors should the company go bankrupt. And it is precisely because of this risk that equity investments produce the highest long term return.

Examples of equity investments are:

$ Shares of a major company, like Royal Bank, McDonald's or Apple

$ An equity mutual fund or ETF (Exchange Traded Fund), and

$ Investment quality real estate, often held through a REIT (Real Estate Investment Trust).

Inheritances

I want to make a special point here about inheritances and the role they play in financial planning as a future asset.

Thinking about them is tricky, as you are dependent on something happening to someone else. In my view, if the inheritance is already on its way to you, as in your grandmother has already passed and the estate is being processed and the amounts are known, then that is an asset you should consider.

If it is merely your assumption that you will inherit something from a parent, family member or friend, then I would recommend you do not put it into your calculations.

Just because someone else has wealth doesn't mean it's going to be yours.

Insurance

Some life insurance policies would also qualify as an investment if they have a cash value component as part of their structure. Life insurance comes in two primary structures: as term insurance or as permanent insurance.

Term insurance is like buying car insurance; you're only buying coverage against a specific risk (in this case, dying) for a specific amount of time. The cost is low as all you're paying for is the insurance against that risk.

Permanent insurance includes term insurance, and then also adds on a savings program so that you actually pay more each month or each year than what the pure insurance costs. The additional amount, or premium, is added to the savings program. In the future, these savings can be used to help fund your retirement, pay for the insurance policy as you get older, or just be a larger nest-egg or legacy that you leave your beneficiaries.

It is absolutely critical to get expert and independent advice when buying insurance.

The premiums and the commissions are low for term insurance policies. And they are much higher on permanent insurance policies. They both have their place – just be sure to get the right coverage for you.

My concern, particularly for young families, is that they put more toward the savings program than they do to buying the right amount of insurance coverage. The risk of dying too early and not providing for your surviving children when they are young is much more serious than worrying about retirement thirty-five years down the road.

Buy the right amount of coverage first, and then save what you can afford. This is usually the right prescription for most people.

Summary – Assets

Now that you have the building blocks for determining your assets, list them.

	Me	Spouse	Total
Lifestyle Assets			
Home Equity (Market Value minus Mortgage)			
Rental Properties			
Business			
Registered Investments (RRSP, RRIF, TFSA)			
Investments Fixed Income			
Investments Equity			
Cash Value of Life Insurance			
TOTAL			

A copy of this form is available at www.recalculatingwealth.com.

What Do I Earn?

When most people consider how much they earn, they primarily think of what they make at work and the numbers on their paycheque. However, you need to have a broader look at all the ways that money comes into the household, both today and in the future.

Income can be classified as either active or passive. Active income comes from actually working. It can be a salary, an hourly wage or payment for a job completed. It is compensation for work you actually did. If you stop working, the payment also stops. In contrast, passive income is paid to you, with little or no effort to receive it. It can be a royalty, dividends, rent, a pension or a government benefit, for example.

It is also critically important to distinguish between what you are paid, and what you actually get to keep. Often, people will view their income as total salary before tax. For example, you may be told by your employer that you earn $85,000 per year. But by the time that gross salary goes through your payroll department and your group benefits are paid, all the government deductions for tax, Employment Insurance and Canada Pension Plan are made – well, you are keeping considerably less than $85,000 per year.

Unfortunately, most people build lifestyle expectations around before-tax income and then pay for them in an after-tax world. This gap is what causes many people to overspend. They are not keeping nearly as much of their income as they believe.

The easiest way to determine what you actually bring home is to add up your net income from your pay stubs from the past year.

Further, how you earn money is important because different forms of income will attract different rates of tax. Employment income and interest income is taxed the most heavily. Money you earn from dividends and capital gains is taxed at a much lower rate, so you keep more of it.

Another consideration is how regular and sustainable your income is. If you work for the post office, your income is much more predictable and longer-term than a professional hockey player, for example. In other words, you need to assess the quality and nature of your income so you understand how reliable it is.

Most people have only one primary income source: employment. Wealthier people often have multiple streams, such as from employment, investments, rent from properties and other business interests. They'll have a number of sources of income that do not necessarily require them to go to work every day.

These sources are also diversified so that if one becomes disrupted, temporarily or permanently, such as a property being without a tenant for two months, they have other places that continue to deliver cash flow.

Most Canadians do not enjoy this level of security. Indeed, if they miss a few paycheques, they are in dire financial trouble. In early 2016, an Ipsos Reid poll found that nearly half of Canadians are within $200 a month of being unable to pay their bills. And one quarter were already behind and unable to cover their current bills and debt payments.

Summary – Income

	Me	Spouse	Total
NET Active Income *Employment*			
NET Passive Income *Rent*			
NET Passive Income *Investments*			
NET Passive Income *Royalties*			
NET Passive Income *Pensions*			
NET Passive Income *Government Benefits*			
Sustainable?			
Ability to increase?			
TOTAL			

A copy of this form is available at www.recalculatingwealth.com.

What Do I Owe?

Our society runs on debt. It is entirely normal that you have a mortgage, line of credit, credit cards, car loan, etcetera. The key is to make sure that both the amount of debt, and your ability to carry it, are within reason.

To manage debt, we first have to look it in the face to not be afraid of it. Dig out all of your statements, and itemize every debt you owe, the interest rate it carries, and how much you are paying toward it each month.

Debt Name	Outstanding Amount	Regular Payment	Interest Rate	Months to Repay
Mortgage	$250,000	$1,000	3%	393
Car Loan	$10,000	$250	9%	48

Next, calculate how long it will take you to pay off the debt. You may need to use an on-line calculator or ask a financial advisor to run the math for you. A quick and dirty way is to just take the total amount of debt and divide it by the monthly payment. That will tell you how many months it will take (ignoring the interest costs).

For example, if you owe $100,000 on your mortgage and you pay $1,000 per month, it will take you at least 100 months, or about 8.5 years to pay it off. A bit longer once we add in the interest payments, but that's close enough to begin appreciating how long you before you are debt free. But interest does matter, so you should take the time, as I did in the example above, to use a calculator and make the numbers more precise.

There are some limits that bankers use to calculate your maximum debt load. They make these calculations when you apply for a mortgage. We can use them here to understand where the outer limits of debt are.

The first is the Gross Debt Service (GDS) ratio. This is the percentage of your income needed to pay all monthly housing costs, which include your mortgage, property taxes, heat and 50 percent of your condo fees, if applicable. The majority of lenders abide by a general standard of 32 percent. This means your GDS should be lower than that to qualify for a mortgage. And if you want be able to eat. ☺ Add all of your monthly housing-related costs (principal, interest, property taxes and heating) calculated on an annual basis), then divide the total by your gross income. The sum is then multiplied by 100 to give your GDS ratio.

Next, we calculate your Total Debt Service ratio. The debt ratio formula calculation is very similar to that of the GDS, except all of your monthly debts are taken into consideration. This includes car payments, credit cards, alimony, and any loans. The industry standard for a TDS (total debt service) ratio is 40 percent.

I should note that while these ratios are industry standard, banks and lenders may use higher or lower ratios when they are making their lending decisions. They will also use other factors, such as your previous credit history and collateral in making their decisions. For our purposes, consider these ratios as guardrails or warning signs. If your debt is near or over these limits, then it must be a priority to reduce the debt ASAP.

There are a few effective ways to reduce debt faster.

Pay the most expensive debt first.

When you listed out your debts, I asked you to identify the interest rate, or the cost of carrying that debt. If you have a mortgage at 3 percent, a car loan at 7 percent and a credit card balance at 19.99 percent, which one should you focus on first? If you made it past Grade 3 math, this should be obvious: the credit card. Yet, I've watched many people scrimp and scramble to make an extra mortgage payment to pay their house off in 8.8 years instead of 8.9 years while their credit card balance stays high and costs them almost 20 percent. And they wonder why they can't get ahead! Pay off your debts in the right order: most expensive gets whacked first.

Pay more often.

There are actually two sides to this advice: first, if you pay extra amounts as soon as you have them, you'll feel more empowered as you are controlling your debt instead of it controlling you. Treat the debt like a misbehaving dog that needs to be corrected regularly. With each extra payment, even a small one, you are demonstrating that you are the Master.

Second, it is a mathematic fact that the debt will go away faster. The reason is that interest is applied to the full outstanding balance and calculated every day. The sooner you reduce that balance the less interest is applied to the debt.

This is particularly true when we look at mortgages which have a long lifespan. If you use a mortgage payment calculator (I'm sure your bank has one on their website, or visit *www.recalculatingwealth.com* and use mine) and play with the Payment Frequency tab. Change it from monthly to bi-weekly (it might be called "bi-weekly accelerated") and watch how much faster the debt is repaid.

Not only are you reducing the interest, you are also taking advantage of a quirk in our calendar. If you pay monthly, you make twelve payments a year. If you make semi-monthly payments, you are making twenty-four payments (12 x 2). If you make bi-weekly payments, you are making twenty-six payments a year (52/2). There are some months where you will actually make three bi-weekly payments in the same calendar month. If you paid semi-monthly, you would only make two.

Neat, huh? This is like discovering your car has an extra gear to help you improve your gas mileage.

Where's My Money Going?

I'm going to outline for you a budgeting formula that actually works, but first let's review the kinds of expenses you have.

I once took a time management course and they talked about taking a bucket, a bunch of rocks and a bag of sand. The goal was to fit all the rocks and all the sand into the bucket. If you put the sand in first, the rocks would not fit. However, if you put the rocks in first, when you poured in the sand it would go around the rocks and fill up all space so everything would fit.

This analogy applies very well to monthly spending. Household budgets are comprised of fixed expenses and variable expenses.

Fixed Expenses – the Rocks

Fixed expenses are the direct obligations that have a long-term nature. They are the regular, recurring bills that you must pay. Some examples include rent or mortgage payments, car payments and regular bills for heat, electricity and phone.

You may also consider other items that are somewhat permanent. For example, if you enroll your kids in sports, then you can consider those costs to be fixed. While the kids may change teams, you still have to budget $500 per month for them and that will continue for as long as your kids play. If you have a car payment, you also know that is going to be a fixed cost, even if you replace the car in the future. If you are helping to support your parents and you have to contribute $1,000 toward their nursing home or care, that's also a fixed cost.

Variable Expenses – the Sand

Variable expenses are all of the little dollars, like tiny sand particles, that you don't seem to notice. But they add up.

If you're like most people, you know what your fixed expenses are, like your mortgage payment or car insurance. But how much you spend at Starbucks, what decorations you buy for your kid's birthday party, that new tie or new purse or that lunch you splurged on yesterday?

No idea.

These variable expenses are the stuff of life and yet most people forget to account for them.

These little items are usually small so it's easy not to notice. A dietician would call them empty calories. Not surprisingly, for many, it is these costs that dominate their day-to-day expenses.

I bet that if you go back over your spending for the past few months, you'll probably find that the little variable expenses over which you have tremendous control are likely out of control and a primary reason for you being off course.

Here's a valuable exercise:

$ Commit to tracking every penny you spend for one month.

$ If paying by cash, get a receipt for every purchase: coffee, newspaper, parking, everything.

$ Relying on your debit or credit cards for as many transactions as possible provides you with an instant electronic record and you won't need to worry about so many paper receipts.

$ Tally these expenses up after one month and I wager you'll have an eye-opening experience.

It might not be possible for you to go back over your spending, because you have no record of these little expenditures. Now that you're aware of the importance of this exercise, you can start paying electronically, collecting receipts, and as soon as one month down the road you can start   gaining   an   accurate   picture   of   where   you   are.

3

Where Am I Going?

"You got to be careful if you don't know where you're going, because you might not get there."

– Yogi Berra

You know you've been off course. But now that you've made sure your emotional baggage stays in the trunk and you've assessed your new starting position, it's time for you to move on to constructive action.

Building a list of the things that are most important to you, and then prioritizing them, is the best next step. You need to have this understanding before you make any changes to your current affairs.

Life is full of changes. The plans you make when you're thirty or forty might not be the plans you still have when you're thirty-five or forty-five. It's okay to change them.

Beware the Paradox of Choice

I've found that many people find the process of goal setting extremely difficult because it requires them to make decisions focused on only a few goals out of many possibilities. And it is this process of selection that is at the root of procrastination.

Picking goals is a trade-off.

Saying yes to one goal necessarily means saying no to others. By not consciously setting a goal and thus picking something to work towards, perhaps many people feel they can keep all of their dreams alive because anything is possible. The rub is that they do not achieve any of their goals because there is no focus.

To get over this psychological barrier, I ask people to make assumptions, rather than decisions. This is far more effective. It's a little less of a commitment, at first, because assumptions can be changed whereas decisions are hard to take back. And as we get moving in a particular direction, the assumption can become more real as we go. It's like seeing something from far away; as you move closer, the details come into focus.

Imagine we're having a conversation about your retirement. You say you'd like to live somewhere warm during the winter months. So, together we need to plan on funding a lifestyle that includes a second home. Now, rather than getting hung up on where the property is (Florida, Arizona or Belize), how much it costs and when you'd go, pick one location as your working assumption and start figuring out how you obtain it. When you get started, all you need is a rough idea, a sketch or outline of the goal. The key is to get moving gradually in that direction. You can figure out the details as you go.

In this example, it's totally fine to say: "I'll assume I'll retire at age sixty-three, spend January, February and March in Florida and I think it will cost me $10,000 each year to do that." Awesome – that's not a full plan yet. But it is an excellent set of assumptions that you can start working with. You can figure out all the other details later – at least now you have a broad idea of what you're working toward.

It's entirely reasonable to check your planning assumptions from time to time. How do you know if they've changed? Look at what you're *doing* – not what you *say* you want to do. And if indeed your planning assumptions have changed, that's okay.

Many times I meet potential clients who say they want to have an early retirement, or to travel or buy a business or some other goal that requires planning and discipline to attain. Yet their behaviour with money each day is not congruent with achieving those goals. If they wanted to save for a comfortable retirement, then they would already be saving. I would just help them do it better.

If you're not adopting the financial behaviours that lead you toward your goals, you need to ask yourself honestly: what are your goals, really?

Sandra's Story

I recently had this conversation with Sandra, a senior executive who works nearly sixty hours per week and is a single mother of two school-aged children. Sandra has a number of competing financial goals: providing her children with a comfortable lifestyle, including private school and summer camps, funding their post-secondary education, and an aggressive early retirement goal.

In building her plan, I guided her to carefully balance her expenses and her savings to make all of those things happen. And it was working.

So I was very surprised when she informed me that she had just bought a larger, much more expensive house. One she can barely afford on her income. It is possible, but it means the kids cannot attend summer camps. It also means that her plan to retire at sixty is over – it's more likely at seventy. So, she can have the house, but the balance requires the kids to stay in the city during the summer and she works for another decade.

Alternatively, she can look to retire at sixty or sixty-five, but with less income than she was planning on. She has decided that a larger home makes life easier every day and she's willing to sacrifice other things to make this happen.

Am I still headed where I want to go?

Recalculating requires that you actually ask yourself: am I still moving in the direction I want to go? If you're not headed in that direction, then perhaps the destination is not what you thought it was.

With all this in mind, let's now develop a workflow for plotting some our key destinations on our recalculated financial journey.

Destinations

A destination can mean many different things depending on what your desired outcome is. Some of the common destinations that people often describe to me are:

$ Enjoying a long, comfortable and worry-free retirement

$ Helping children financially

$ Helping to fund grandchildren's future education

$ Assisting parents in their later years, or

$ Leaving a legacy to a charity, church or cause.

There are no right answers: these are your goals and your potential outcomes.

> **The most important thing about destinations is that you are emotionally connected to them.**

Your destinations are initially painted in broad strokes. Either you are interested in them, or you're not. The destination is the ultimate goal or goals you are working toward. You may never get there, but each step you take, each twist and turn, should lead you closer to it.

Scoping Out

Once you have identified your primary destinations, and set up some assumptions for what they look like, it's important to start to make them real in order to achieve them.

When I ask people about their primary goals and destinations, they often have trouble articulating them. So, we work through a process of identifying working assumptions, as I mentioned earlier. It's like creeping up on the goal-setting process. It's making a small decision to defer the big decision. It's a good first step because at least your feet are moving.

But if the destination is not one that you have strong feelings about – maybe it's actually someone else's destination of choice and you're going along for the ride, or maybe you think it *should* be a goal but it doesn't set your belly on fire – then you will not remain committed to it. It will remain an idea that you don't get much traction on.

Your goal or destination must have specificity if it is to be realized. It needs to be measurable. It needs to be real. And it's even better if it's in full colour. It's the difference between saying: "One day I'd like to travel to Europe" and visualizing the details as you taste a glass of wine in a Tuscan vineyard or smell lavender in the purple fields of Provence.

Let's try it. Imagine that you say you want to go to Paris. Can you get an image of the Eiffel Tower into your head? What else can you paint into the picture with you?

Where will you visit?

When will you go?

What will you pack?

Who will go with you?

What will the weather be like?

Do you want to live like a local or travel like a movie star?

Will you stay in two- and three-star hotels to be cheap and earthy, or do you want five-star luxury?

Can you see the city in your mind in the morning? Can you see it all lit up at night?

What will the food taste like? What will it smell like?

What will the ride up the elevator in the Eiffel Tower feel like? Scary? Exhilarating? Can you feel it moving underneath your feet now as you imagine it?

If you close your eyes and think about the actual experience of visiting Paris, you probably want to go right now, don't you? If you've already been, then perhaps you're ready to go back and revisit, while specific memories dance in your mind.

If you had no interest in Paris, then you probably didn't participate in the exercise. :-)

The mind is an amazing tool. The more real you can make the goal in your imagination, the more you can visualize it, hear it, feel it and smell it, then the more likely you are to achieve it.

Napoleon Hill said, *"Whatever the mind can conceive and believe, it can achieve."* I've found this to be very true, in my own life and in the lives of my clients.

In short, we need to move from "someday" to "what day?"

Waypoints

A "waypoint" is a stopping place on the journey to your destination. In some cases, reaching a waypoint is necessary for you to reach the final destination.

A waypoint is the thing you want to see, do or achieve along the way. Some waypoints are for you, things you do for yourself, and some are things you want to do for other people.

Examples of waypoints would be:

$ Paying down the mortgage and being debt free

$ Buying a vacation home or cottage

$ Taking a luxurious vacation, or

$ Buying an expensive item, such as a fancy car, boat or jewellery.

For many people, life is all about moving from one waypoint to another. Waypoints add richness and purpose to life. This is important. Because if you can identify those important lifestyle goals, you'll find that most of these waypoints take time, planning and money to achieve. They are unlikely to happen by chance.

It's also true that reaching the waypoints impacts arrival at your final destination. If you spend too much time or money on the waypoints, you may never get there. For example, spending too much money on new cars and annual vacations means you are not setting aside enough money to fund your retirement plans. You may be sacrificing your future lifestyle to enjoy today. Indeed, this is a key challenge I see all the time with new clients.

Bob and Jacqui

Bob and Jacqui illustrate this point very well. They are both highly successful and extremely capable business people. They have high incomes and enjoy a comfortable lifestyle. A beautiful home to raise their two children, a new cottage to enjoy and new cars in the driveway. In short, they've worked hard to have a wonderful life.

Yet, they are not saving nearly enough to support this lifestyle when they are in retirement. In our most recent conversation, the focus now turns to identifying what their ultimate destination is (comfortable retirement, helping their children to be educated and established and looking after aging parents) and examining what the trade-offs need to be. Can they spend a bit less on some expenses today to make sure they can cover what retirement is going to cost?

The fact that saving for the future is essential may seem obvious.

In today's world, delayed gratification is a slow internet connection.

The message about saving can indeed be a tough sell.

I have also seen the opposite situation, however, where people save more than they need instead of enjoying more that life has to offer today. This can happen out of fear, out of habit or out of an unexpected change in financial circumstance. My late client Betty was an example of all of these.

Betty's Story

A child of the depression, Betty grew up having to get by on very little. A modest upbringing led to a modest lifestyle as an adult. One of the key lessons she learned as a child was the value of having a steady job and a regular paycheque. With this as her paradigm, she began her working life as an operator at Bell Canada. She progressed modestly up the corporate ladder, never showing a lot of ambition, but delivering solid and reliable performances every day. She was shy and never one for excitement, danger or risky pursuits. She didn't travel, had a few life-long friends and loved her cats.

The one thing relevant to recalculating that Betty did really, really well was save.

Betty saved reliably and she saved well. As an employee of Bell Canada, she began participating in the staff share-purchase plan as soon as she was eligible and continued until her mandatory retirement at age sixty-five. She reinvested most of the dividends and let the shares accumulate and grow for over thirty years.

When I met Betty in the late 1990's, she had 19,130 shares of Bell Canada Enterprises (BCE). I remember the exact number as I had to count all of the individual share certificates when she took them out of her safety deposit box. When BCE subsequently spun out Nortel Networks on a 1:1 share basis, she received 19,130 shares of Nortel. For a woman who had never in her life earned more than $60,000 per year, by the spring of 2000 she was worth almost $6 million.

Betty had more wealth and more dividend income than she knew what to do with. She would not spend it, would not enjoy it and would not give it away. She had never travelled, did not have a drivers' license or a passport. I remember calling her in the summer of 2000, during a particularly hot spell, to see how she was doing. To keep cool, she was spending the day sitting in her bathtub. Her small house in a working-class neighbourhood in Toronto had no air conditioning. And she was not interested in spending the money to install it. Despite my efforts and arguments, Betty would not spend what would have taken less than 0.1 percent of her portfolio to be comfortable on the hottest days of the year.

When Betty passed away in 2014, I attended her funeral. There was a small gathering of old friends and co-workers there to remember her. She had left her estate to her closest childhood friend's children, who lovingly called her Grandma Betty.

She was buried as though she was penniless. I'm sure that as they stood on the well-worn carpet in the local funeral home and paid their respects to Betty, in a pauper's casket made from cheap particleboard, they had no idea the tiny, gentle lady who cared deeply but quietly was actually quite wealthy. I would have loved to be there when her lawyer read the will and they discovered she was a multi-millionaire who had bequeathed them a fortune.

Betty lived the life she wanted and passed away peacefully and happily. Along with her laugh (more of a girlish giggle, really), I'll always remember that phone conversation, of her cooling off in her bathtub while my computer screen says her account is worth more than five million dollars.

Milestones

As you move from waypoint to waypoint, you need to track your progress. By identifying key milestones, you can keep moving in the right direction and see how far you've come and how far you still need to go. To be useful, the milestones must be visible, significant, and placed wisely along your journey.

Milestones are different from waypoints. A milestone is a mark of your progress as you go. A waypoint is an interim destination you selected along the way. They might mark the same spot as a waypoint in some instances – like paying off the mortgage – but they do not need to be.

Visible

A milestone is a roadside marker that lists the distance to a particular location. To be effective, you must be able to see it from far away, and in all weather conditions – particularly fog.

A key milestone might be an annual income target, such as making $150,000 per year by age forty-five. Or it might be paying off the mortgage and being debt-free by age fifty-five, so that you can approach retirement with one less worry. It may also be buying your first house, taking a special vacation or finishing a university degree.

To be useful, the milestone must be specific, measurable and well placed. Think of it like speed limit signs. You don't find them behind a tree, in small script and in colours hard to read at night. They are big, reflective, easy to read and placed right where you can see them. That's what your milestones should be.

It's also important that you know what they look like before you see them. This comes back to why you should write down key goals in advance. If you can visualize them, and tell yourself the story of why they're important – to the point that you can make them real in your mind and feel how it will feel to achieve them – you have a much greater chance of reaching them.

Every sports coach will tell his or her athletes to visualize their ideal performance. *Seeing is believing* starts in your own mind.

In his book, *The Success Principles*, Jack Canfield asserts that consistent visualization causes three things to happen:

1. It programs your mind's reticular activating system to start letting anything that will help you achieve your goals into your awareness.

2. It activates your subconscious mind to create solutions for getting the goals you want.

3. It creates new levels of motivation. You'll start to notice you are unexpectedly doing things that take you to your goals.

Visualization is not mind over matter. It is mind *with* matter.

It is about adapting or training your habits to naturally and automatically act in the way that your mind has trained it to act.

Successful visualization is not achieved in one session. Like a muscle, it gets stronger with use. When you consistently repeat thoughts, those thoughts become impressed into your subconscious. Your brain becomes trained to automatically send signals to the body to act in accordance with those thoughts. Visualization brings those thoughts out of the realm of the subconscious and into the conscious.

Here's an exercise to help you visualize your goals.

$ Write out your key milestone.

$ Collect some images that reflect them. For example, if a key milestone is to buy a house, then find a few photos that represent the ideal house you'd like to buy.

$ Print out the photo and put it on your bathroom mirror so you see it every morning. Make it the wallpaper on your phone and the screensaver on your computer. Put one on your refrigerator and next to the phone on your desk.

Everywhere you look, you'll see your goal right in front of you. This will help you stay focused on what you want, when other things start competing for your attention. You're less likely to book a holiday or make an impulse purchase when you are so focused on what you really want.

Significant

A milestone should also be a significant event in life, like graduating from college or getting married. Along with being something you aim for, a milestone is a marker that allows you to reflect on where you stand in life.

The key is to have targets that matter and that are congruent with your ultimate goal and destination. They should be big enough that you stop and celebrate them, big enough that you check in and take stock of how far you've come. Reaching a milestone can result in a decision to change direction or a renewed commitment to the road you're already on.

It is also quite common for there to be a significant emotional element to reaching a milestone. If you've ever had the experience of getting something that you've worked for, you'll know what I mean. If it was challenging, then there's a sense of relief and pride of accomplishment. This is an awesome feeling and it can fuel your tank to drive you forward to another, higher goal.

Or maybe it's not as much of a thrill as you thought. Perhaps it was too easy. Maybe the finish line didn't feel like the accomplishment you expected. It can also leave you with a void. You're not where you wanted to be or you didn't get the outcome you were expecting. So – what's next? This is very common when people reach retirement and the three-month holiday period comes to a close.

Milestones can also take you by surprise, meaning that an event can happen to make you appreciate just where you are on our journey.

I had just such an experience a few years ago. My wife Sue and I were planning to take a cruise holiday for the first time without David and

Olivia, our kids. David was ten, and Olivia was six – old enough to stay with grandma for a few days while we took a few days off from being Mommy and Daddy. This was one of our milestones.

A month before our departure, Olivia was hit by a car in front of her school. Every prayer I've ever made and will ever make was answered and she suffered only very minor injuries. But we were terrified by how close we came to losing her.

Suddenly, the idea of having a holiday just as a couple was not what we wanted. Being together, holding each other and celebrating just how wonderful our lives were right at that moment was the only thing that mattered. So, without regard to cost (and it was remarkably expensive) we booked, at the last minute, three additional airline and cruise tickets to take the kids and Grandma with us. Recalculating indeed.

Where Have I Already Been?

It's also helpful to consider and understand what you've already accomplished, what you've already done and what you have not yet been able to do. Perhaps there are waypoints you didn't get to, no longer want to get to, or that don't exist anymore.

Ralph and Gwen

For example, clients Ralph and Gwen told me several years ago they wanted a cottage. They desired a second home, where they could enjoy the summer months in peace and tranquility. Buying a cottage was a key destination for them. They have friends who have cottages and, while they've enjoyed visiting, they really wanted to have a place of their own.

We outlined the goal in great detail and defined their ideal cottage: where it would be, its key features, the approximate cost and annual operating expenses. With this target in mind, we identified a specific savings rate and schedule. It took almost three years for the plan to unfold, and they found their perfect cottage. It was precisely what they were looking for. Mission accomplished.

Two years later, they informed me that the cottage was up for sale and I could expect to see the proceeds reallocated to their retirement plan.

"You worked very hard to get this place, and you've only had it for two summers! Why are you selling now?" I asked.

"We discovered we're not cottagers."

I wasn't sure what that meant, so I asked for more details.

"Well, we love the idea of a cottage, and we love going to our friend's cottages. But when you visit for a week at a time, it's not the same as having a cottage for 52 weeks of the year. Ownership is not the same experience."

Ralph and Gwen proceeded to give me a rundown of their challenges: constant maintenance, rising property taxes, lost battles with mice, the mystery of septic tanks and so on.

Another client, Kevin, sold his business in his forties and was looking forward to an early retirement and a comfortable life on the golf course. Only three years later, he was starting another company. As it turned out, while he was able to golf every day, none of his friends could. They were still working. While he had reached his goal, he found that he had few people to share and enjoy it with.

Kevin, Ralph and Gwen discovered that sometimes getting there isn't always what you thought it would be. Arriving doesn't mean finished.

Reviewing your past destinations and waypoints can give you great insight into what you really want. And considering other opportunities might make you change your mind about the path you're currently on.

Serial Versus Parallel

Allow me to deviate for a moment into a brief discussion of basic electricity. I'll use a strand of Christmas lights for my example.

A serial circuit is one where if one light bulb goes out all the lights go out. Each light is wired to the next one and all must work for each one to work.

A parallel circuit has all of the lights wired together, but also independently from each other, so that if one light goes out, the other lights can stay on.

This concept is important because from time to time we see clients who believe that their financial planning should look like a serial circuit. They must achieve one goal or waypoint, before moving on to the next one. In their minds, they have constructed some kind of order or sequence that must be followed for them to feel comfortable that they're achieving their plan.

Marvin and Jesse

Marvin and Jesse had exactly this view when I first met them. A young, successful professional couple, they had a young family and a list of specific goals to achieve. They wanted to be mortgage free by age 40. They wanted to have private school education for both their children. They wanted to take nice vacations each year and see the world with their family. They wanted to enjoy a very comfortable retirement by their late fifties. They had great jobs, were disciplined savers and figured they should be able to achieve everything they want out of life.

Their challenge was they couldn't figure out how to put all the puzzle pieces together to make it all happen.

When I reviewed their situation to understand their current state, I discovered that almost all of their uncommitted cash flow was going to pay down their mortgage. There were only token amounts being saved for their children's education, family vacations and retirement plans.

When I asked them about this, they both agreed that paying down the mortgage as quickly as possible was the central assumption in their planning. They were looking at all of their desired destinations and waypoints as if they were part of a serial circuit. Once they had paid off the mortgage, they would move on to addressing their other plans.

I pointed out to them that they could do that. But the achievement of that milestone or waypoint (to be mortgage free) meant they could not, at the same time, put their children in private school, take annual holidays or make tax-advantaged contributions to their retirement plans. So, they could indeed be mortgage free at an early age, but they would not have accomplished any of their other goals. And they could not get the time back.

I showed them that if they dialled back on the mortgage payments and reallocated the funds to their other goals they would be able to achieve everything they wanted – but the mortgage would be paid off a bit later than planned. They would be mortgage-free by age fifty instead of age forty (and still before their planned retirement) and they would have educated their children and enjoyed wonderful trips each year.

After reviewing our estimates and projections, they decided that our plan gave them a richer journey. They would have better balance by doing a little bit of each part of the plan than by focusing all efforts on each part, one at a time.

Fuelling the Tank

Another advantage of reviewing your past destinations and waypoints is to remind you of the distance you've already come and accomplishments already made. This can be a very empowering experience.

In my experience, most people have accomplished more than they give themselves credit for. If you think back to what was materially important to you ten years ago, for example, and where you thought you would be today, are you ahead of where you thought you would be? What challenges did you experience and overcome? What still remains to be worked on? What successes have you had, and what did you learn so you can have more of them?

I suspect that most of us are harder on ourselves, more critical about ourselves, than we probably should be. An honest assessment of how far you've come may help you realize that you have more success, more creativity and more stamina than you thought.

Take a few moments and step back from yourself and your current situation. Look at you from a distance, as if you were outside of yourself. Play a game: you're meeting yourself for the first time and hearing your life story. What would it sound like? What were the challenges this person had to bear, what were the circumstances they had to deal with? Did they have passengers they had to pick up along the way, what detours did they have to take and what obstacles did they overcome? Whom do they love, and who loves them? What are they most happy about, and what do they hope to achieve next?

As part of this review, you'll likely find that some factors and events were external, beyond your control. You'll also find that some outcomes were a result of your own behaviour and were conscious decisions on your part. In short, what did the world throw at you and how did you respond to it?

If you were to write your own story in this way, what would it look like? What would such a conversation sound like? How would you feel at the end of telling it?

Most of us are focused on the right now and what's coming next. Life moves pretty fast, and we don't stop long enough to look around. If you did not get where you thought you were going to go, then some honest, introspective analysis can be very helpful.

There is little to be gained by beating yourself up over past mistakes, just as there is little to be gained by taking too much credit for what may have been pure luck. Let me give you a tale of the latter.

My first multi-million-dollar client won the lottery back in the late 1990's and went from having $30,000 to her name to $5.8 million in her bank account. While I was busy creating a plan that would give her and her children a lifetime income and pay for a wonderful lifestyle, she wanted to start trading high risk securities and taking options on bio-tech stocks. And this was just as the tech bubble was forming. She thought she was a savvy investor because she had lots of money. It was almost impossible to remind her that Warren Buffett did not become successful because he had the right Quick Pick. Indeed, she had already enjoyed the best return the universe could possibly provide, turning $1 into nearly $6,000,000. How much more did she think she could get?

As I watched her make one bad financial decision after another, it was clear to me that we had to end our relationship. She was not interested in my help. I haven't spoken with her since before the tech wreck, when the NASDAQ went from 5,132 in March 2000 to 1,114 in October 2002. As the vast majority of high risk technology stocks were wiped out, I'm fearful and saddened to think of what might have happened to her.

So, in this case, had she honestly reflected on her fortunate outcome and let her balance sheet expand rather than her ego, she would have built a robust portfolio and resilient financial plan that would still be performing for her and her children today. Knowledge is empowering, and evaluating what has led us to where we are now, and comparing it where we want to go, is essential to changing behaviour.

It is this recognition of your own power, that you are indeed in charge of your own destiny and that you have come farther than you thought, that fuels the tank to take you further on.

No Blame, No Shame

Reflecting back on your journey so far can be a very emotional process. I suspect that this is precisely why people often avoid it. It is easy to begin blaming or shaming yourself or others for any negative outcomes and this can be a huge barrier to planning moving forward.

No one wants to admit that they may have failed, that they are unable to overcome a challenge, so avoidance becomes a learned behaviour. The good news is this confrontation is the most critical step towards understanding. When you look at your past decisions, you must do so honestly and say to yourself or your partner: "Look. We are where we are, it is what it is. Let's learn what we can and then move forward."

And, as in the example of the lottery winner, you cannot take too much credit for good luck either.

Remember, this is really a process of recalculating and recalibrating. Just as the GPS unit doesn't get mad at your for missing a turn, you'll be better served by taking the emotion out of it.

No judgments. No blame and no shame. You're plotting a new route now!

Who's Going with Me?

Another key item to address before you get back on course is to understand who is on the journey with you. Who else must you consider in your planning? Who's in the car as you set out, and who might you need to pick up along the way?

Start with your immediate family and then think up, down and sideways.

First Class Passengers

These people are already in the car and on the journey with you. You need to consider their needs first, as you are financially responsible for them and their outcomes. Your spouse and children would be your first class passengers.

First class passengers have priority; their needs come first and your entire journey is built around them: where they want to go, how they want to get there and their comfort along the way.

Should the needs of one of your first class passengers change, then the entire journey might need to change to accommodate them. If they want to stop and see a sight, then you all stop and get out. If they want to make a side trip, or buy souvenirs along the way, then you likely need to change the plan to make that happen.

It is important that everyone in first class has consensus about the journey. Before setting out, you need agreement on the destination and the route, so that everyone knows how long the trip will take, what they can expect along the way and what it looks like when you get there. Making everyone in the family part of the process helps avoid the "Are we there yet?" questions.

In most families, each person has a different destination in mind, different roads they want to take, speeds they wish to drive. It's extremely important you negotiate together how you're going to deal with these differences before you set out.

For example, I work with one family where one spouse is a pension fund manager and the other is an institutional trader. I'll call them Derek and Valerie. They are obviously financially savvy and very successful. They really do not need my help in managing their investments with respect to strategy and picking stocks. However, despite their business acumen, they are almost incapable of identifying how much money they need to save for their daughter's university education over a decade from now.

It's not that they can't do the math. They can. It's that they cannot agree on how much they wish to intervene financially in her education. Derek says that he put himself through school, working part-time while studying, and struggled for years to reach his goal. And it is precisely this struggle that he feels gave him the discipline and drive to be successful in his career. He would like his daughter to work just as hard as he did, so she may also fully value her success in the future.

Valerie, on the other hand, feels that they should help their daughter as much as possible economically, so that she may put her full time and attention to her studies. Valerie says that Derek wasn't noble – he simply had no other option as his parents could not afford to help him. Because they *can* afford to help their daughter, it is their duty as loving parents to do so.

Left to their own devices, Derek and Valerie's car wasn't going to leave the driveway. While they had some agreement on the ultimate destination – their daughter's education – they could not agree on exactly where they were going or how fast to get there.

Fortunately, I was able to help Derek and Valerie recognize the issue and ensure they heard each other. A compromise was struck and we starting moving forward with a plan that each of them agreed on. A specific amount of money is now being set aside regularly so their daughter can have a great start – but not a luxurious future.

Second Class Passengers – Going Up

If your parents or in-laws are still alive, consider to what degree you will become responsible for their care, either directly or indirectly. And even if they have sufficient financial resources to remain independent, what might be the impact on your time to look after them physically or emotionally?

In most families it is the female spouse who becomes the primary caregiver for the couple's parents on both sides. In other words, it is usually the eldest daughter or daughter-in-law who assumes this role. The job is urgent, uncompromising and consumes tremendous amounts of time and emotional capital.

As part of your planning, you need to make an honest assessment of how you may be helping your parents now and in the future. This assessment needs to be financial as well as emotional and physical.

For example, it's one thing to identify how much an in-home caregiver will cost. Or the monthly cost of a suite in an assisted-living facility. But the cost to be available and "on call" to an aging parent, to take them to doctor's appointments, grocery shopping or just for companionship, is almost impossible to forecast. Yet it is something we must try to anticipate and be ready for.

It's also important to consider how your plans are intertwined with your parents. Are you all engaged in the family business? Do you own a cottage or home together? Do you owe them money? Do they owe you money?

I quite often work with people whose family shares a vacation home or cottage, owned by the parents and enjoyed by all. While it may be the parents' desire to leave the home to the children, there are a multitude of considerations and questions that come up. Who will pay the taxes when the parents die? Will all the children want to co-own the property together? Can they contribute equally to the annual expense and up-keep?

You also need to see if there are other family members who can support *you* in this regard. What if something happens to you? Who could come to your aid in a financial emergency?

Coach Passengers – Going Sideways

To what extent are you involved with your siblings and other family members? Are you financially engaged with them? Is that possible in the future?

Frequently I see siblings that are identified in the will and power of attorney documents for potentially important roles. It is common that each spouse will appoint the other as their Executor or Estate Trustee. If they are unable to act, they usually appoint a brother or sister as a contingency. If you've done this, you now need to ensure that your sibling is actually able to help manage your affairs or your estate if your spouse isn't able to do it. Do they live in the same city? Are they good with money and financial decisions? Are they willing to do the job? And have they appointed you in the same role? If so, would you be willing and able to act? Are you the guardian for your nieces and nephews?

And are there other family members you might need to rely on, or might rely on you? An aunt or uncle, a cousin or step-child? A good friend of mine and his wife have adopted her nephew because his parents have substance abuse problems and cannot properly care for the child.

Once you've considered family, what about close friends? Or causes you care deeply about? Have you considered how you might want to include them in your planning? You might consider not just who is in the car with you today, but who may be in the future. There are also things you may be interested in that give you satisfaction spiritually, emotionally, intellectually: causes or institutions you care deeply about such as your church, alma matter, a charity or political party.

Hitchhikers

Financial hitchhikers are people you might encounter who require your help to get where they're going. There is always potential for someone, perhaps a friend or family member, to ask you for financial help. When this happens, you'll have to make a decision to either stop and help them, or let them fend for themselves and continue on your way. Sometimes they jump in front of you, and sometimes you can see them on the horizon from a long way off. In any event, you'll need a plan to deal with financial hitchhikers before you encounter them. You can only put so many people in the car and so much luggage in the trunk.

In some cases, they are going the same way you are, and helping them is a minor inconvenience. Indeed, helping a loved one can be rewarding in its own right.

However, if helping them means trailing too far off your own course, to the point where it puts your plans in jeopardy, then this becomes a very serious decision.

For some people, their financial car broke down and hitchhiking is a temporary solution. With your help, they can get going again.

But for others, hitchhiking is just their normal way of getting around. If you don't slow down and pick them up, they'll just catch the next car coming down the road. Knowing the difference between the two is critical!

Write It Down

Once you've completed the review of past destinations and you're feeling confident and empowered about the future, it's time to envision your most important outcomes from the perspective of your ideal self.

The most important step in this process is to write down your goal, in as much detail as possible.

We know that people are far more likely to achieve a goal that is written and specific, rather than vague and fleeting.

Writing down your goal makes it real.

Adding details makes it distinct and help to connect you to it emotionally. Remember the vision of Paris?

People often tell me they are planning for a comfortable retirement. To make this a reality, I ask them to paint a picture of it, or ask them to tell me a story of what that retirement would look like. I ask them to make it real in their minds, and then tell me what achieving that comfortable retirement would feel like. Can they describe what they'll be doing, where they will be, who they will be sharing it with, what it sounds like, what it smells like. I want them to incorporate all of the senses. The mind is an amazing tool and if you can make that reality exist in your mind, then your brain can decide it's possible in real life. It goes from being just a dream to a waypoint or destination.

This process of visualizing, hearing and feeling your goals in vivid detail brings you much closer to achieving it. I recall one of my University professors telling me that about ten years after graduation, I'll make within 10 percent of what I think I'd like to make. In other words, if I thought when I left school I'd make $100,000 per year in ten years or less, then I'd make between $90,000 - $110,000. I've canvassed several of my old classmates, and this indeed seems to be holding true for many of them. And perhaps it's true for you too. So when you set your goals, aim high!

I've also found this phenomenon to be true when I ask people about their education plans for their children. The more specific I can get them to be, the more invested they are emotionally in having it happen. The more I can help them put structure around it, the greater success my clients have experienced.

The conversation sounds like this: "You say you'd like to help your daughter attend university. OK, which university? What course of study are they most interested in? Can we download a course calendar from their website and see what the tuition and books will cost? What about accommodations? Will she commute to school, stay in residence or rent somewhere else? What will that cost? How about food? Transportation? Will a new computer or other items be necessary to acquire?"

Once we have this destination scoped out, we can compare it to where they are right now. How much has already been saved? In what kinds of accounts and investments? How long until she goes to school?

Next, I help them calculate the distance from here to the goal in the time they have to get there. What they need to know is how much more they need to save, in some combination of lump sums and regular savings, and at what rate of return to get there.

It's like when you go on a trip, you need to know how far it is, and how fast you need to drive to get there within a certain period of time. You can then also calculate how much gas you're going to need so you don't run out before you get there.

In chapter five, *What's the Shape of My Retirement?* I'll give you the process for running the math on your primary retirement plan.

Before you get your calculator, there are two other important considerations to make.

The first is that I want you to ask "why there?" or "why that goal?". Knowing your *why* is extremely important. The *why* is about your relationship with money, what you have learned about money and what you believe about money. Is achieving this goal just a fleeting idea, like watching the latest Cialis commercial, or is it something you've dreamed about since childhood? Are you aiming for a retirement lifestyle that you really want, or do you think it's one your friends will also have?

When you plan, you need to know how committed you are and how emotionally invested you are in achieving the goal. Will you drive the way you need to drive to get there? Or will you change destinations or give up part of the way when something else becomes more interesting?

The second consideration is that you should treat this process of goal-setting as establishing a set of working assumptions, not permanent decisions. As we've discussed already, assumptions are easy to create whereas decisions are hard to make. And it's important that you just get going on your journey and make adjustments on the road rather than wait until you have everything decided upon before you set out.

There's no point in having the car packed and being afraid of leaving the driveway because you haven't mapped your every second of the journey. Life has movement; you'll make course adjustments as you go.

4

Habits for a Successful Trip

"No matter where you go, there you are."
– Buckaroo Banzai

Now that you've figured out where you are, where you're going, and you have an idea how to handle the major challenges and detours you're likely to experience, it's time to focus on how to drive well towards your destination.

Staying out of trouble in the first place is best. And I've found that there are a few key behaviours, tips and tricks that people who are good with money employ, and those who are lousy with money do not.

Pay Yourself First Isn't Working

North Americans are not considered to be the world's best savers. According to a report from KKR & Co.[2] in 2014, China earned that title

---

with a savings rate of over 40 percent. Germany and France were also in the top five with 17 and 15 percent respectively. The United States and Canada were well below 10 percent.

The traditional advice from financial planners is *pay yourself first.* The idea is to put your savings as the first and most important item in your budget, rather than leaving it to the end after all the other bills are paid. The implementation is straightforward: identify a specific savings amount, say $500, put it aside and then pay all of your monthly expenses on what is left.

Doing this reminds me of the advice for how to lose weight: eat less and exercise. Easy to say, but hard to do. If *pay yourself first* was as easy to do as it is to recommend, then Canadians and Americans would have dramatically higher savings rates.

What most of us actually experience is that once all of our monthly bills are paid, there is nothing left to save. Savings is a luxury for when we have excess cash flow.

I believe the reason for our failure to save in this way is actually a noble one. The problem with *pay yourself first* is that it does not align with how most people feel.

Paying ourselves before we live up to our other commitments seems selfish and irresponsible. Making sure the household bills are paid, food is on the table and our family is looked after are our first priorities. We put other people ahead of ourselves – and in particular our future selves. Indeed, we don't save because we *are* responsible!

So while many of us are not considered to be good savers, we are very good at paying our bills. And to really learn to save, we need to capture that emotional reality that we are responsible and disciplined and change the view that saving is a luxury that comes when we're done managing all of our other financial commitments.

Bill Yourself First

If you change how you think about something, you can change how you feel about it. And if you change how you feel about it, you can actually change your behaviour. So, if you decide to think about *savings* as another bill, you can change how you feel about it.

Consider your targeted savings amount as a bill that you must pay for your future self. It's a bill that your future self has sent to your current self that must be paid.

Billing yourself first is not discretionary and it is not selfish.

Indeed, it is essential that you pay it before all other current expenses so that you and your family actually have the future you want and need.

If we assume a 10 percent savings rate (about what the average Spaniard saves), then put 10 percent of your paycheque into your investment or savings account as soon as you get it. This is very easy to set up as an automatic transfer with your bank. And if you treat it as a bill, which is mandatory, rather than as savings, which feels discretionary, then you will actually do it and stay with it.

10/70/20: The Best Budget Formula

So, now that you know how to identify your expenses, and understand that the variable costs are ones we have a high degree of control over, you need some guidelines for managing them.

Most traditional budgeting techniques do not work because they are too much like dieting: they are seen as an uncomfortable project. While most of us can diet for a short period of time, it doesn't become a habit because it's hard. We feel deprived, and it's not sustainable. But if it's going to work, we need it to become a habit.

If you've ever run out of gas, then you know the best way to avoid it happening again isn't to track your mileage, it's to fill up the car as soon as you get to a quarter tank. That's an easy habit to follow and doing so avoids the problem.

The best template I've found for establishing – and following – a monthly spending program is the 10/70/20 plan.

The First 10 Percent

The first 10 percent of your income is the money you put away for your retirement. This is the bill from your future self that your current self must pay. This money is squirrelled away in registered savings vehicles, like RRSP's, and TFSA's and is best invested in long term assets like the stocks of the world's best companies and high quality real estate.

The Next 70 Percent

The next 70 percent of your income is to pay all of your current day-to-day living expenses, both fixed and variable. This pays all the household bills, the gas in the car, the food on the table, lunches and dinners out, internet bills, dry cleaning, everything.

The Final 20 Percent

The final 20 percent is used to pay down any short-term debt, like that perpetual credit card balance or the student loan. It can pay down that debt for the hot tub or the boat. It can also be used to fund extraordinary expenses, like the trip to Punta Cana or the new iPad you bought your daughter for her birthday.

Once these are done, and there is no more short-term debt, this 20 percent allocation builds up a cash reserve so you have a buffer for all those other incidental expenses that come with life that are outside our normal and expected costs.

For most of us, the first task is getting our current lifestyle costs to fit within the 70 percent limit. If you track your spending for a month or two, you'll likely find that this can be done by paying closer attention to your variable expenses. Watching the pennies, and forgoing a few unnecessary purchases is often all that is necessary to gain control over your spending.

If you can get your 10 percent put away as soon as you get your paycheque, and next figure out how to live on 70 percent of what you make, everything else pretty much takes care of itself.

	Target	Actual	Difference (+/-)
10 percent for long-term saving			
70 percent for living expenses			
20 percent for short-term debt or cash reserve			

A copy of this form is available at www.recalculatingwealth.com.

Sticking to the 10/70/20 plan for monthly expenses is critical. The best way to make sure you save is to set up automatic monthly withdrawals from your bank account to your savings and investment accounts. If your 10/70/20 plan calls for say, $500 per month to be put away for your long term goals, and you are paid bi-weekly, then have $250 deducted from your bank account the same day that you get paid. If the money doesn't stay in your regular account, you won't spend it. Take the savings out of the rotation!

> **Remember: _Bill_ _Yourself First!_**

Another way to ensure you are saving at an adequate pace is to be sure to maximize your contributions to tax-deferred accounts. This is an excellent milestone because if you can make your maximum RRSP contribution and your maximum TFSA contributions, then you are likely saving enough to fund a comfortable retirement.

If you're not able to save enough, then perhaps the problem lies elsewhere. It's true that actions speak louder than words. If you say you want to have something in the future, and yet you seem to live only for today, then you really don't want what you say you want. Your behaviour must align with your goals.

If you're finding that it isn't, then perhaps you're not being honest with yourself about what it is you really do want. This sometimes isn't a math problem, it's a behavioural one. Take a good long look in the mirror and ask yourself what it is that you really want. Figure out what it is and then own it.

Conduct a Fire Drill

What would happen if your partner didn't come home one day? Or the doctor told you that the spot on your x-ray wasn't operable? Of you fell down a flight of stairs and couldn't work for three months? Or ever again? These things happen every day and to very nice people – just like you. And most have no plan for them.

To assess your readiness, conduct the planning equivalent of a fire drill. Create a list of questions and then figure out if you are prepared with the answers. You have this huge database between your ears: have you backed it up somehow?

Here's a short list to get started:

$ Do I know where my insurance documents are?

$ Have I run some calculations to ensure I have enough money in case my partner dies?

$ Would we have enough if one of us wasn't able to work again?

$ Do I have a will? Is it current? When was the last time I reviewed it with my lawyer?

$ Do I have a valid power of attorney? Is the person I appointed the best choice?

$ Have I left a list of all my accounts (bills, investments, banking, etc.) along with the relevant passwords so someone else can access them?

$ If most of my life is stored on my phone, does someone else have the PIN so they can access it if I can't? What if I lose my phone?

$ What about my online profiles? Who will cancel my Facebook/Twitter/Google+ accounts?

When I engage clients in this conversation, I've discovered a number of interesting things. First, they seem most keen to discuss this after they've been to a funeral. They've just been sitting there, looking at a box or an urn containing the remains of someone they've known and cared about, and they're thinking, "One day I'll be in there. What's my family going to do?", or "My spouse will be in there. What am I going to do?" I guess it's only human that we consider our own mortality when we're in the presence of death. And we realize that no matter what happens, life carries on.

Practice Driving

Another thing I see is that each partner in most couples don't have the same driving skill. By this, I mean that each has a sphere of responsibility within the household and the other spouse has only a passing awareness of those responsibilities.

It is very common that one will look after the bills, and another will handle the investments. One is more comfortable in the kitchen, the other in the garage. One mows the lawn, the other tends to the garden. So, a key part of your planning is to identify who does what, and ensure that the other is able to handle those tasks to the degree they are comfortable, because someday they might have to on their own. They don't necessarily have to learn to do the tasks themselves, but they do have to have a plan for getting those jobs done. So, if only one spouse drives, and that spouse dies, then the survivor needs to either learn to drive, get a bus pass or open an Uber account.

Finally, I've also noticed that perhaps just 30 percent of people who come to us have their wills and estate plans in order. And about only 10 percent have it done well and keep their plans current. Family situations change, tax laws change, family law changes, so your plans sometimes have to change. Sadly, most of the time a proper risk management and insurance plan is being treated as a luxury when it is indeed a necessity.

I'll also point out that this is one area where there is no DIY solution. If you're over eighteen, have a job, have some assets and, in particular if you're married and have children, then you must obtain qualified, professional advice to get your estate plan in order. It's not hard, but it does cost a bit of money and some time to accomplish. And doing so is both responsible and necessary.

If you're unable to communicate, for example if you're unconscious in hospital, the power of attorney gives someone else the ability to help you. You'll need two kinds: one for your money and one for you. The power of attorney for property gives someone else the authority to look after your financial affairs, such as paying your bills and addressing your investments. The personal power of attorney will appoint someone to speak for you in regards to your medical treatment, what you wear, eat and how you're looked after. Both documents are essential and usually prepared at the same time by your lawyer. You can appoint the same person to both jobs, or split the responsibilities between different people.

You Don't Build It, You Just Drive It

One of the least helpful pieces of advice I hear about money is that you should only invest in things you understand. If this advice was applied to your daily life, consider how you would move through your regular day.

Do you need to know how electricity works to turn on the lights or the coffee maker? How does the internet work? Elevators? Anti-lock brakes? What is toothpaste made of? And what, exactly is in that hot dog you're having for lunch?

It should be self-evident that to function in our modern world, we simply cannot understand how things work. Even if you are an expert in one field, say medicine or plumbing, you are not an expert in every field. The key is not understanding how things work – it's understanding how to work them.

Let's use Tylenol as an example. If I have a headache, I know that if I take two pills, it will likely be gone in a little while. Do I know how it enters my blood and changes my body's chemistry? Nope. I don't have to know how Tylenol works. I just have to know how to use it safely. Taking the entire bottle with a Vodka chaser is probably a bad idea. Leaving the bottle open if I have young children in the house is also not smart. If my doctor tells me not to take it because it will interfere with my other medications, then I won't. Apart from that, I'm fine to take the product and count on it working for me.

How does my cell phone work? No idea. I can't text while I drive and it won't work underwater. My monthly bill is also beyond my comprehension, by the way. Do I put my phone down until I can appreciate the electronic magic that allows for this amazing communication tool? Of course not.

Unless you have a graduate degree or professional certifications in finance and extensive experience in the securities industry, the vast majority of quality investments will be hard to understand. They're complicated. If you only want to buy the simplest of investments, then you will deprive yourself of many terrific and suitable opportunities.

Knowing key investment principles is important, from the perspective of safe and effective usage. You're the driver, not the mechanic.

Here are some key things you should know about your investments so you invest well:

- $ In plain language, what is it supposed to do?
- $ How does it make money? When is this most likely to happen?
- $ How will it lose money? When is this likely to happen?
- $ What is the expected return?
- $ What is the potential loss?
- $ How likely are either of those?
- $ How it is it taxed?
- $ How does it fit into the rest of my portfolio? In other words, does it play well with others?

$ Is it making my portfolio better? How?

$ How do I monitor it so I know it's still working for me?

$ When and how do I sell it?

$ What does it cost? Is that reasonable?

You should be able to answer these questions about every investment you make. And if you can, you'll know more about your portfolio than 99 percent of investors.

5

What's the Shape of My Retirement?

"A journey of a thousand steps begins
with a ~~single step~~ cash advance."

– ~~Lao-Tzu~~ Darren Coleman

A warning: the retirement calculations you are going to make will include an implicit assumption that is false. That assumption is this: whatever amount of money you want to have and spend at retirement will remain so, adjusted for inflation, for the balance of your life. It simply doesn't happen that way.

Retirement calculations falsely assume that the road ahead of you is a straight line.

So, you need to know that if you want to have $50,000 per year for life then that is how the software will make its calculations. Without considering fluctuations to deal with life.

I also find that this is how people think about their retirement income goals, if they think about them at all. (And they certainly do not consider the impact of inflation, as I will discuss shortly.)

It is human nature to project directly straight ahead − because we cannot see around corners, and we're not from the future, so we don't know all the new things that are coming at us.

However, we know that life is never a straight line, so all we need to do is consider that as we're planning. Life brings surprises, challenges and opportunities that we must address.

When you plan your retirement, you must also build flexibility around your income expectations.

While you cannot see everything that is coming, there are some broad assumptions that you need to decide on that will have a significant impact on your mathematics.

For example, in my experience, many people like to front-end-load their retirement with travel. They plan for the first five-to-ten years of retirement to be when they are most active, as they feel they are the most robust and can count on their health. The view is that they will start slowing down as they reach their mid-seventies.

I then point out to them the high cost of health care that they are likely to experience in their eighties and nineties.

Now, the rough outline of their future retirement income is not a straight line, it's a curve that goes up, down and then up again.

It's called the bathtub curve as it looks like the sides of a bathtub.

When thinking about your own retirement, it would be helpful to consider how the bathtub curve may shape your expectations.

My 7-Step Retirement Income Planner

Let's assume you want to have a retirement lifestyle that today would cost $50,000.

You plan to retire in twenty years and have already saved $250,000 towards you goal. Further, you can save $1,000 per month towards your retirement goal.

Explanation	Sample Calculation	Sample Result
Step 1: How much? (Current dollar terms)		
If you were retiring today, how much will you need annually from investments to sustain your lifestyle?	$50,000	$50,000
Step 2: How much in the future? (Impact of inflation)		
What will this be in future dollars when you retire? *(Assume at least 3% annual inflation)*	($50,000 x 1.03)$^{20 \text{ years}}$	$90,305
Step 3: How much at retirement?		
The total you'll need to have at retirement to withdraw from at a rate of 5% per year	$90,305 x 20	$1,806,100
Step 4: How much saved now?		
Money saved in whatever form (RRSP, TFSA, cash, etc.)	$250,000	
Step 5: How many months to retirement?		
Let's take your annual numbers and make them into monthly numbers	20 years x 12	240 months
Step 6: How much can you save each month?		

Explanation	Sample Calculation	Sample Result
Thinking about all the things you buy monthly, how much can you set aside to add to your retirement accounts each and every month?	$1,000	$1,000/mo.
Step 7: What ROI will close the gap?		
What rate of return will you need to close the gap?	* See below	0.066 or 6.6%

*Using a business calculator where: N = 240, PV = (250000), PMT = (1000) and FV = 1806100. *Solve for "i".*
A copy of this form is available at *www.recalculatingwealth.com.*

Once you've completed your planner, go back and change the variables until it works. If the ROI calculated in Step 6 is above 8 percent, then you'll have to go back and adjust your variables. Either plan to spend less, save more or work longer.

Running the math

As you work with your own numbers and try to land on a good travel plan for your retirement destination, you can play with the three key variables (distance, speed, and time) to come up with the combination that suits you.

Distance

Is the goal too far or too close? What you're looking for is the numerical amount that you're trying to reach, the amount of money you need to have at a particular point in time to reach your waypoint or destination. If you've calculated that you need $1.5 million at age sixty to retire comfortably, and you have $750,000 now, then your distance is to another $750,000. This is your milestone.

As Sharon discovered after she bought the new house, the distance to her milestone increased. When we meet Charles and Pamela in chapter seven, *Staying on the Road*, we'll discover that they were actually past their goal and had saved more than they needed. While Sharon's goal was now further away, for Charles and Pamela it was too close!

Speed

The rate at which you can save and invest will dictate the speed you can travel. Your progress will be a mix of how much you put away and how much that savings earns as it grows.

If you assume that you need your portfolio to grow by, say, $20,000 per year, and you can only save $15,000, then you're asking the money to work far too hard. There's no way you can drive the portfolio that hard or that fast. You'll crash or blow the engine. The amount you can save and earn needs to be reasonable. Just like when you drive, there are speed limits you need to obey.

If you want to stay in the slow lane and drive as safely as possible, you'll need to save far more money. Because you'll be working harder than your money does.

If you want to save less, then you're going to have to learn to drive in the fast lane and stay right at the speed limit. You'll need to either be a great driver, or hire one to get you there.

For most people, the best idea is staying in the middle of the road and earning moderate returns while saving diligently. Yes, other cars will pass you from time to time, and some of them will be driven by your brother-in-law or best friend. Don't be jealous just because they seem to be going faster. You need to go at your own speed. Also, respect that even though you're staying out of the fast lane, you can still have a flat tire or fender-bender occasionally. Driving is not a risk-free activity.

When running your math, assume a 2 percent rate of return for the slow lane, 5-6 percent for the middle lane and 8 percent for the fast lane. But I caution you, the math looks better at 8 percent obviously, but few people are skilled enough to get that without having an accident. Or two.

If you're going to drive in the fast lane, then you also need to accept that you'll see about 30 percent of your money disappear every decade or so in a bear market. There is no avoiding this. It's a statistical reality.

If you drive in the middle lane, you can expect to see a 10 percent decline every ten years, with 5 percent declines every two to three years. Staying in the slow lane will keep you out of trouble with minimal chance of even a 5 percent decline. You'll find you may be reasonably safe, but you won't get there. As the comedian, Steven Wright famously said, *"Anywhere is within walking distance if you have the time."*

One of the ways you can drive faster is to make the car lighter by getting rid of baggage. When you examine your monthly expenses, are there things you're paying for that you don't really need? If you pack lighter, and take on fewer monthly costs, then you can save more aggressively and get to your destination sooner. If the engine runs leaner and is more efficient, it needs less gas.

I should note that people will often drive at a certain speed based on their previous experience. If they've never had a crash, then they may drive too fast. If they've had a crash, then fear of having another one may make them drive too slowly. It is the same with investing. People will invest based on their emotional experience rather than on the mathematics of what their plan requires. In other words, they will invest based on fear and greed, rather than on prudence and wisdom. I often find that people's risk tolerance in investing is coloured by either their worst or best financial experience. If they've lost money before, then they are going to look at every investment like it's going to happen again. And if they've had a big winner, then they keep looking for the next lucky jackpot.

The best example of the latter I've seen is with another advisor I know. While he may be responsible in managing his client's money, his own portfolio is fraught with risky stocks and venture capital ideas. When I asked him why he gambles with his own portfolio, he told me how one lucky stock pick years ago went so well he was able to pay off his house. Ever since, he continues to hunt for the next big winner. Instead of considering his previous success like a winning lottery ticket (which it was), he attributes it to a fortunate event that he is destined to repeat. Despite his training, education and experience, his emotions lead him to bet rather than invest.

Like Edison inventing the light bulb, who said he found 10,000 ways that it didn't work, my colleague sees every investment loss as just another step towards his next big win. There's no telling him that lighting almost never strikes twice.

Time

How long will it take to get there now? This is the next variable to either calculate or establish. If you want to retire in fifteen years, then that is your 'time'. Alternatively, you can identify how much you want to have in the future, how much you have now and how much you can save, then you can calculate how long it will take to hit that goal. Does the math say you can get there in fifteen years? More? Less?

Marvin and Jesse discovered that taking a bit longer to reach retirement meant they could see and do more along the way. More waypoints meant arriving at their final destination later but with a more meaningful and enjoyable journey. Sometimes, speed isn't everything.

Everyone Ready?

Now that you've created a set of goals or planning assumptions, you need to check if your plans are realistic. Not just mathematically realistic, but emotionally realistic.

Unless you're travelling alone, are you sure that everybody involved agrees with where you're going and how you plan to get there? And are they ready to go when you are? What do they want to see along the way? As we found with Derek and Valerie and their plans for educating their daughter, their original planning speed bump was not a math problem, it was an emotional one. They both agreed on the destination, but had wildly different ideas about how to get there. Figuratively, Valerie wanted to drive their daughter to school; Derek wanted her to ride her bike or take the bus. My solution did not provide a set of financial projections or an investment strategy, it was to mediate a dispute.

Sheila

I have another client with potential challenges on the horizon. Sheila is a very successful corporate executive. She has had a stellar career and her performance has led to increasingly more high profile roles. Her current position puts her on a global stage and her reach is only increasing. Her husband, Brent, has taken responsibility for their home and raising their children and ensuring that their domestic life is just as successful as her professional one. When asked, Brent feels that Sheila will retire in the next few years, and enjoy a very comfortable, peaceful and well-earned retirement.

Having not had a chance to discuss this topic with Sheila (her schedule is such that we almost never see her), I suspect that given how her career is accelerating, she may have a very different view. Indeed, she has recently been lured away to another firm for an even higher profile position. Her star is still ascending. I don't think she sees retirement coming in the same way as Brent.

Taking Two Cars?

I've also found that sometimes, in a planning sense, it's better to take two cars. If each spouse has their own income and assets, and they cannot agree on how to drive or all the stops they want to see, then it can help to craft two different plans that intersect along the way. I've had to do this only a few times in my career, but the frequency is picking up, and particularly among couples that are in second or third relationships. They've had the experience of being stuck in the car with someone else before, and they now put a premium on their freedom and independence.

Donna and Ralph

For example, my clients Donna and Ralph are both divorced and planning for retirement in the next two years. While not married, they have been living together for the past few years. They split household expenses and enjoy travel, golf and curling together. In the winter, Donna would like to spend three to four months in Florida to escape the long Toronto winters.

Ralph, however, has two grandchildren from his first marriage. Both boys are active in hockey and Ralph enjoys coaching the younger one's team and being the loudest spectator in the stands for his oldest grandson. For him, spending more time with his grandchildren, and particularly as they enjoy his favourite sport, is a central part of his retirement. So, while Donna has no desire to be in cold hockey rinks all winter, that is exactly where Ralph wants to be. And for Ralph, there will always be sunny beaches and warm sand. But his grandkids are only young once.

Each has their own retirement plan, but we've helped them appreciate that their plans are not mutually exclusive. Indeed, a compromise is not far away. Rather than feeling that each is dependent on the other and both are unhappy, we've found a way forward that allows them to be interdependent and enjoy their own retirement dream.

Donna will enjoy the early part of the winter, golfing with her friends in Naples, while Ralph focuses on coaching the kids' budding hockey careers and being the best grandpa around. He will travel to Florida for the holidays and celebrate Christmas and New Year's Eve with Donna. Donna will travel back to Toronto to cheer the boys on during their playoffs in March and April. Donna will cover the expenses for their condo in Naples, and Ralph will manage the costs of maintaining their townhouse in Markham. And each will pay for their own plane tickets back and forth.

With respect to their financial plans, we determined a reasonable budget for each, rather than one budget for both. This respected the uniqueness and independence of their respective lifestyles, and also their autonomy over their own assets, as each brought their own money into the start of the relationship. We then applied some reasonable assumptions about inflation and other costs, and then calculated the rate of return each one needed to achieve in their portfolios to generate the income necessary to retire comfortably, *and stay comfortably retired.*

Do We Have Enough Gas?

Note that I've emphasized *stay comfortably retired.* It is essential to look at how expenses and costs may rise over time. In my work, I need to calculate not just how much money you'll need in the first few years, but also what your lifestyle may cost ten and twenty years down the road.

When you run the math of a retirement plan, you must realize that the ultimate goal is always moving.

Life has movement, markets have movement and prices have movement.

Figuring out what your own goals are, and then having the discipline to cost them out properly is hard enough. You must also consider that all the things you want in the future will cost more than they do today. You don't want to run out of gas just as you see the sign for Disneyland.

The historical rate of inflation has ranged from 2 to 4 percent. Indeed, most central bankers around the world use this as their acceptable range of inflation. This means that prices will double roughly every fifteen years.

A challenge for most people is that this number is too general. It applies to an array of products and services, some of which you may or may not need in retirement. Unfortunately, while technology is making some items less expensive (for example, the iPhone7 does more and costs less than the original iPhone, so that reduces inflation), most of the things we will buy every day will likely rise in cost more quickly than that. Food, gasoline, health insurance, property taxes, dinner out: all of these become larger and larger components of your monthly expenses in retirement. So, it follows that your personal inflation rate may be somewhat, or even considerably, higher than the broad government estimates.

To ensure you don't run out of gas, it's essential that you build a reasonable inflation rate into all of your projections and forecasts. I use 3 percent for my clients. While you could argue that's high, particularly when the government is telling us there is no inflation, my view is that this provides a degree of safety in our planning. I would also counter that there are expenses you have today that someone who retired years ago didn't have. For example, what was your Netflix bill in 1997? You didn't have one.

Where are the Gas Stations?

Along with determining how much gas you have now, and identifying important milestones and waypoints to measure your progress, as discussed in the last chapter, you also need to know how to get more gas as you go.

Life is expensive and the idea of saving before you reach your goals is a bit old-fashioned. Your grandparents may have abhorred debt and saved to pay cash for their cars, vacations and even their houses. They only used credit cards, if they had any, in emergencies.

That's a far cry from today's delayed gratification, which is a slow Google search. We live in the *right now*, not ten years from now. The news cycles are accelerating and Amazon will soon be able to deliver your next purchase of toothpaste by drone helicopter, thirty minutes after you order it. I would argue that for almost everyone born after 1965, the idea of putting money away for the future does not align with any other experience they have in their lives. It's like canning vegetables, stocking firewood or changing your own oil. It's old fashioned and cute.

As we discussed earlier, *paying* yourself first doesn't work. People are just not saving enough. So, for many, it is unlikely that they have saved enough to get them all the way through retirement. If you don't have enough gas at the start of your journey to get you there, you'll have to figure out how to get more wealth along the way. The good news is that, unlike gas, cash seems to be a renewable resource.

Bonus at Work

The first gas station is a bonus at work. Most people think of their annual bonus as part of their total income, and theoretically it does form a key component of your compensation package. However, I would like you to plan your day-to-day expenses around your regular income, and use the discretionary bonus you may receive as an extra boost of capital that you can use to top off the savings tank. Don't count it, and don't spend it before you get it. And certainly don't blow it on something frivolous.

Sell Stuff

The second gas station is where you can sell some things you no longer need or want. Are there assets you can sell that will also give you more capital? Can you dump something from the past to help you with your future? E-Bay has become the internet version of a garage sale. You likely have items you're no longer using (electronics, furniture, boats, etc.) and would be better converted into cash to fund other goals. If you're lucky, maybe you're sitting on a treasure of old hockey cards, comic books or Star Wars action figures that a collector would pay handsomely for. Get paid to empty your basement.

Inheritance

Another gas station that most people look for is a future inheritance. If our parents or close relatives are still alive, then it's reasonable to think that some of what they have may become ours in the future. No one likes to own up to this view, but many people share it.

Let me repeat my earlier comments: I encourage you to eliminate any potential future inheritance in your planning. First, people are living longer than ever, so mom and dad may have their house and cottage for much longer than you expect. Second, elder care is becoming astonishingly expensive, so this might consume much of the inheritance you're expecting. Third, this is a morbid idea. Fourth, if you tell me about it, and mom dies, it may be considered motive. I don't want to share my notes with the cops ☺. So, take my advice and plan for your own life.

Downsize

As you approach retirement, a significant form of unlocked capital becomes your primary residence. Indeed, many people assume they'll sell their house in the city at retirement, unlock the proceeds and move to a less expensive home, perhaps in another area. Who needs four bedrooms when the kids have gone?

Again, I caution my clients to think about their home as a lifestyle asset as much as it is a financial asset. Unless this is a central commitment in your retirement plan, to sell, unlock equity and move, my view is that you consider it a final option when everything else has been used up or other strategies have failed.

Go Solar

A solar powered vehicle has, in theory, the ability to keep going indefinitely. It doesn't need to stop and get gas or plug in to get charged. It keeps moving by generating its own power with the sun. The changing nature of work and the amazing capability of technology allows people to keep working and staying productive for as long as they choose. Who needs to go into an office, when you can access the internet from your laptop in a beach chair? Work can now follow you. If can morph, change and be as flexible as you can make it.

An extreme example of this can be found in Muskoka, Ontario at Kevin O'Leary's cottage. You may know Mr. Wonderful from his roles on CBC Dragons' Den and Shark Tank as well as his regular appearances in financial media on TV and radio. Kevin seems to be everywhere – and where he really likes to be is at his cottage in Muskoka, Ontario.

I was enjoying a beautiful August day at his cottage in the summer of 2015, and while I was there, he did live TV segments on BNN and CNBC, all from a mini-TV studio he has built into the den off his cottage living room. The technology is such that he can run the camera, lights, sound and remote broadcast by himself, while wearing a jacket and tie above his bathing suit. Kevin has made his work come to him. Wonderful, indeed.

Defining retirement not as the end of work but as the beginning of a new relationship with work is becoming easier for many retirees. You can work on your terms, at your convenience, and it is an opportunity rather than an obligation.

One of the more interesting developments I'm seeing in newly retired clients is that they continue to work, but shift the balance of work and play in a very dynamic way. They may enjoy two weeks on a cruise, or practicing for a golf tournament, and then take on a consulting project for six months. This keeps their minds stimulated, their skills sharp and the project funds their next holiday or fun expense.

Buying Gas

Risk is fundamental to investing. It is impossible to have any meaningful discussion or interpretation of returns and investments without putting them into some context of risk.

The challenge for most investors is figuring out what risk is, where risk really lies and what the differences are between low risk and high risk.

Most investors assume that volatility, or how much something moves up and down in price, is the best measure of risk. But fluctuation is not the same as loss so it is an unreliable measure of risk. It's like flying in an airplane and mistaking turbulence for a plane crash.

Another definition of risk would consider the likelihood of an investment experiencing a permanent and total loss of value, which can be avoided through reasonable due diligence and proper diversification. Yet another would be the security underperforming some kind of benchmark, such as the Standard & Poor's 500 (S&P500) or Dow Jones.

I would caution that this is as helpful as comparing your cholesterol to your neighbour who runs 5K every morning.

My personal favourite definition comes from Warren Buffett, who famously said, *"Risk is not knowing what you're doing"*. This applies equally to driving, home renovations, gas barbecues and investing.

My driving metaphor provides some help in thinking about categorizing investments. When you pull up to the pump at the gas station, you're confronted with three choices for fuel: regular, mid-grade or high octane. Each has its own unique benefits: regular is low cost and sufficient for most engines. High octane is the most expensive, delivers greater engine benefits and is often recommended for higher performance vehicles. Mid-grade suggests a balance between the two.

And so it is when you select investments to fuel your investment portfolios.

You can categorize most investments into similar categories as gasoline, organizing them by regular, mid-grade or high octane risk.

Regular

Most investors would be comfortable owning investments in this low risk category. They are predictable, preform reliably and are useful for a wide range of investment applications. They are also of reasonable cost and easily accessible. Examples include guaranteed investment certificates (GICs), term deposits, government bonds, most fixed income bond and mortgage mutual funds. Key features include a guarantee of paying you a fixed amount on a regular basis as well as the return of your original investment at some future point.

Indeed, these are the favourite choices of most savers. And please note my word choice: savers. *Savers are not investors.* Savers want predictability and favour guarantees over anything else. They avoid even the merest whiff of risk and feel that even a five-year term deposit to be an aggressive investment. You are trading the risk of future uncertainty for the guarantee of price and return today.

While these low-risk investments provide a drama-free investment experience, the primary drawback is that they also deliver a low level of performance. They provide poor mileage. Indeed, most investors will not reach their goals by filling up their portfolios with low-risk investments. They do not deliver enough energy potential to take you all the way there and you will run out of gas before your destination. You will either have to start out with more gas than you thought, keep filling up the car, go slower or decide to stop earlier.

There can also be a further performance penalty if these investments are held outside of a registered account like an RRSP. As they primarily earn interest income, they are taxed at the investor's highest marginal tax rate. So not only do they pay the lowest amount of income, you pay the highest rate of tax and keep the least. This tax is like extra wind resistance that slows down your savings and ruins your mileage.

Going too slow is expensive.

High Octane

At the other end of the spectrum we have higher risk investments that are intended to provide greater growth at the expense of higher volatility or fluctuation. Growth investments can fuel your portfolio to run a bit hotter and a bit faster. The benefit is that you can get better mileage and go farther with the gas you have in the tank. The investment portfolio, the engine of your financial plan, works harder so that you don't have to.

A high-risk investment is one where there is either considerable potential for loss of capital or underperformance, or a relatively low chance of a devastating loss.

If you were told that there is a 50/50 chance of your investment performing as expected, you would likely consider that to be moderately risky. If there was a 95 percent chance that it will underperform, and a 5 percent chance of success, you'd likely also consider that to be risky to the point of speculation. That would be a lottery ticket.

The reverse of this is a large chance of success with a small chance of devastating loss. This is important, and explains why many people are afraid of flying in an airplane despite it being the safest way to travel. There may be higher likelihood of being in a car accident, but also a high probability that I'll walk away uninjured. Not a lot of people survive a plane crash, even it if happens rarely.

As an investor, you need to plan for what is highly probable, not what is remotely possible. You can buy insurance for the catastrophic risks. I shake my head each time I see someone smoking nervously outside an airport terminal. They're more afraid of the airplane than they are of getting cancer. Statistically, the safest place for them is inside the airplane where they can't smoke.

And so it is with high-risk investments. Rather than viewing them as pure speculation, you should put your focus on finding higher growth investments. Not lottery tickets, but seeds that you plant today so you can sit under a shade tree sometime in the future.

Examples of high-octane investments include rapidly growing industries or countries. You need only look at the amazing developments taking place in wireless technology, health care, electric cars, or telecommunications to realize that some prudent investments in these areas is a wise decision when planning for your future.

Emerging markets also demonstrate this dynamic. Look at the skylines of Shanghai, Seoul, Dubai or Ho Chi Minh and how they have changed in the past twenty years to appreciate what high growth economies can deliver. Yes, they are volatile but they are growing fast. Just like teenagers. Seriously, search Google for images of the Shanghai skyline from the 1990's and today. You will not believe it's the same city.

It is this volatility that presents the primary challenge for investors. You can see the long-term opportunities of these investments and how they can help you – the trick is not to get scared out of them.

Going too fast is dangerous.

Mid-Grade

This is Goldilocks' category. Not too cold and not too hot. Just right. As it is for most engines, mid-grade or moderate investments are often the best choice for most portfolios. They are optimized for decent performance and fuel economy at reasonable cost.

A compromise exists between some growth and reduced volatility.

If we couple this with a focus on more reliable, higher quality investments and a dedication to diversification, the risk of a devastating loss is dramatically reduced.

The chance of not reaching your goals is also less as the overall rate of return should be higher than with low risk investments.

From my perspective, the key challenge with mid-grade investments is when markets are running at extreme temperatures. When we are in a temporary market correction, people become highly risk averse (some are terrified) and the growth component of their portfolio is losing money. They want to exit those investments and rush to the low risk ones.

I see precisely the same behaviour in reverse when we're at the top of bull markets and investors feel they are not earning enough. The low risk portion of their portfolio feels like riding the brakes, dragging down their overall performance. So, to catch their bragging brother-in-law, they want to sell the securities that provide ballast in a storm so that they can go as fast as possible.

Both behaviours are signs of an emotional disturbance rather than a prudent investment strategy. Even if you have the right kind of gas, you still need to know how to drive.

The first rule of investing is: don't lose money. The second rule is: buy low and sell high. By dumping your excellent investments when they are down you are violating both rules. You turn a temporary fluctuation into permanent loss. And you are selling low when you should be buying, and buying high when you should be selling. You are rebalancing in exactly the wrong way at precisely the worst time.

Selling your moderate investments to load up on risk and chasing an inflated market is also a bad idea. Yet I keep seeing this movie and somehow people seem to forget that it always ends in tragedy, not comedy. I've watched it with the Asian tigers emerging markets in the early 1990's, technology stocks before Y2K, flipping real estate in the early 2000's, gold in 2009 and social media stocks today.

The great benefit of a moderate portfolio is that I can adjust the balance between low-risk and high-risk investments to create a customized approach for each investor. If you're young and have a long time before you need the money, you can accept more fluctuation in your portfolio, so you should be tilted more towards growth investments. If you're nearing or in retirement and need to start taking income from your portfolio, but you still need it to last for another fifteen to twenty years, then you need more precision and more predictability in your outcomes. So, turning the dials back towards more income-oriented and more stable investments would be appropriate.

By paying attention to how much you need and when you need it, you can dial up or down the risk/return scale so that the portfolio moves as you move.

An easy example of how to accomplish this is with a balanced mutual fund. There are some that are considered income-balanced funds, where the mix may be 60 percent to low risk investments and 40 percent to high risk. A neutral-balanced fund would be 50/50. A growth-balanced fund would be 40/60. A properly trained and experience advisor can help create a tailored plan for you.

Preferred Routes

With a GPS, you can select the type of route you prefer to take with common options being fastest, shortest and recommended. Not only can you choose your destination, you can also choose the style in which you get there.

Fastest Route

In a financial planning context, I see the fastest route option as one that would mean living frugally and saving very aggressively. Not a lot of room for luxuries. The attitude would be to sacrifice current comfort for a better future lifestyle.

Now, just like trying to drive very fast to get where you want to go, you may arrive quickly but you've also missed seeing a lot of stuff along the way. You took the highway rather than the back roads and didn't take the time to stop and smell the roses. By focusing intently on getting to where you want to go you will have to give up some of things that give life colour, flavour and texture. When I think of Betty sitting in her bathtub in the summer, this is precisely what I envision as the risk of getting there too quickly. It just doesn't have to be that way.

In my experience, people who choose the shortest route, who maximize thrift and eschew luxury, do so not because they have done the math and want to retire as early as possible. Rather, it stems from an emotional issue where living with less, and perhaps having a greater sense of independence from financial concerns, is their driving force. In some cases, it arises from living with frugal parents and the habits are passed down. I've also seen it where the parents were spendthrifts and spent every dime they ever had. Growing up with nothing in the cupboards, either because there was little to be had or daddy spent it all at the track, is a powerful memory and one that can shape behaviour as an adult.

Shortest Route

When you select the shortest route, you're likely to be modifying an earlier destination that now looks to be too far away. The focus on reaching the closest goal may become more important than maximizing the richness of the goal. For example, if your original plan was to retire at sixty, you may now decide to retire at age fifty-five and live on a bit less. With less time to save for the goal, there is less capital to save until you need it. And once you start withdrawing, you'll need that money for a lot longer.

This is a common option when people see their employment situation change in their mid-fifties. With a severance package and early retirement suddenly before them, their original plan is suddenly much closer, even if it is a bit less than expected.

I recently had a chat with an old friend who had just been 'retired' from his employer after over twenty-five years of service. This came as a surprise to him, as he hadn't planned on fully retiring for at least another decade. However, with a generous severance and a healthy pension entitlement, he has decided to embrace the opportunity to retire now and focus on his hobbies, his family and building a cottage. With ten years less to save, and ten more years to spend, his lifestyle will be more modest than he had expected, but he's happily traveling economy class now and enjoying the luxury of time.

A change in health can also mean the shortest route is best. My late father was diagnosed with a terminal heart condition many years ago which led to his early retirement. With an uncertain timeline ahead of him, he decided to travel and see a bit of the world while his health remained strong. He also undertook a project to build a family history to share with our relatives. He enjoyed his final years spending time with old friends, collecting photographs and sharing stories with family across the country. Once he knew his time was limited, his focus was on squeezing as much as he could out of what he had left.

Recommended Route

Finding the ideal balance between living for today and planning for the future is the best outcome of great financial planning. Just as the GPS unit will balance speed, time, distance and traffic to select the optimum route, so it is with planning our personal financial journey.

Let's return to our earlier example of Marvin and Jesse with their original plan of taking the fastest route to retirement. As we discovered, doing so meant they would miss a lot of wonderful experiences with their family along the way. When I worked with them to plot a course to reach their goals in parallel rather than serial fashion, I showed them that the fastest route was not the most enjoyable.

By moving their retirement date back a few years, and taking a bit longer to pay the mortgage off, they would have more cash flow to travel with their children and to afford their private school education.

After I showed them the math, they discovered that doing more now, and getting to their other waypoints a bit later, was indeed the best solution.

Unfortunately, I more commonly see the reverse situation, where people are using up all the gas right now and will not have enough to get them to their destination.

A very sad example I have recently encountered is with a professional athlete who is nearing the end of his playing career. He has discovered, too late, that a lifetime's amount of income has slipped through his hands in under a decade. He has made millions, spent millions but unfortunately has not saved millions.

His previous financial advisors took advantage of his trust, lack of knowledge and attention and lined their own pockets well.

Along with poor investment advice, they also failed him by not addressing his spending and allowing him to live a lifestyle that he cannot possibly afford once the paycheques from the team stop. He does have a good retirement pension from his player's union, but he must wait twenty-five years before he can begin collecting.

Had he been coached years ago to find a better balance by spending less so he could enjoy longer, he'd be looking at a remarkably comfortable lifestyle once his playing days are over. I suspect we have been brought into his situation too late to fully overhaul his math problem.

6

Getting Underway

"The secret of getting ahead is getting started."

– Mark Twain

With your working assumptions for milestones and waypoints figured out, some guidance for how to get there, and now that you're in the car, gassed up and ready to go, it's time to hit the road.

Driving Lessons

New drivers have the most accidents. Driving is complicated and a lack of experience can be very dangerous. It's the same with investing. I've found, not surprisingly, that our best clients are the most sophisticated and experienced investors. If you're new to investing, or have had more than a few accidents in your portfolio, then get help. Read some personal finance books, hire an advisor and stick to the fundamentals. Don't go out on the racetrack until you've mastered backing out of the driveway. Parallel parking and making safe left turns may look easy but they're not.

Even long-time drivers can benefit from a skid-school or a course in advanced handling to sharpen their driving skills. As an investor, you can never stop learning.

Good drivers appreciate risk. To properly discuss risk, we need to have an acceptable working definition of risk. For most people, risk is defined as 'losing all my money'. This is not really the risk that investors should be afraid of. Rather, they should be more afraid of outliving their money or their lifestyle costing more than they have. Being broke at eighty-five because you spent all your savings and then asking your kids for money is truly risky.

Understanding Your Risk Tolerance

I've found that there are two much better definitions of risk. The first is: risk is not knowing what you're doing. This applies to investing as well as to skydiving and gas barbecues.

Learning a skill can reduce risk.

The second definition I like is that risk is a lack of robustness. Risk is fragility. Think of a rickety ladder. Things that are built well are rarely risky. Their quality construction makes them stronger. A big, new Mercedes is safer than an old moped.

When investing, both of these criteria can reduce risk. Investing prudently means building a carefully constructed portfolio of quality investments, and then owning it well. But the former is easier than the latter.

Buying a balanced mutual fund from one of the leading investment companies will accomplish the former. Yet having the discipline to hold it during a market correction or a bad news day when everyone around you seems to be panicking? That takes some skill, experience and discipline.

What separates good investors from bad ones isn't their investments, it's what they do with their investments that makes all the difference. So, if you are not – or do not – wish to be skilled at building and managing a solid portfolio, hire someone to do it for you. If they're good, they will be worth their weight in gold.

When I ask clients about their risk tolerance, I'm like a doctor taking their temperature: I know where it ought to be but I need to check if they're running too hot or too cold.

Most often, having them invest according to how they feel at the time is a recipe for disaster. Most people are aggressive and over confident at the height of bull markets. And they are most fearful at the bottom of bear markets. As humans, we have a psychological bias towards presuming that what has just happened will continue to happen. It's called extrapolation. If things are bad, we assume they will keep being bad. And if they're going well, we feel upbeat, positive and confident that the sun will keep smiling on us.

So, if you're feeling very bullish and aggressive, it's likely because markets have recently been strong. I thus need to make your portfolio more conservative than you might want in order to protect you from a future correction. Conversely, when markets are in a trough, you may feel terrified that another drop is just around the corner and want to hide your money in the mattress. That is the precise time you should invest more actively and buy things when they are on sale.

Experience & Training

New drivers crash more. As they have little experience, and minimal training, they drive poorly and do not assess risk well. Either they drive too slowly because they are terrified or they drive too fast and recklessly because they don't know any better. They confuse excitement with success.

Remember, if risk = not knowing what you're doing, then learning to drive reduces your risk. Speed does not equal recklessness. Driving too slowly and never taking the car out of first gear means your journey will take much longer than you thought and require lots of gas. So, if you invest too conservatively, you'll either take too long to reach your goals or you'll never be able to stop saving. If you drive too fast by investing too aggressively, you'll crash often and your portfolio could be fatally damaged.

You don't have to work too hard to become a better investor. There are many books on the subject and Warren Buffett's shareholder letters *(found at http://berkshirehathaway.com/letters/letters.html)* are like a Master's degree in great investing.

The fastest and best route is to find an excellent financial advisor.

Along with teaching you, a good financial advisor can coach you regularly to ensure your investment behaviours are as intelligent and successful as your investment portfolio.

Changing Speeds & Cruise Control

I've been asked how people can change speeds once they've started. In other words, can they affect a material change in their planning by going slower or faster, or taking a longer route instead of a shorter route. Can they save more, spend less and retire later?

I believe you can. But only if you have help.

Becoming a better financial manager is a lot like becoming more physically fit. How do you lose weight and improve your cardio? Eat less and exercise. And if it was just that easy, we'd all be hot.

If you want to have a better diet, that means you're probably eating poorly now. To eat better, you're going to have to get someone to show you how.

If you don't exercise, then you probably don't have a regular workout routine or know your way around a gym. To train without hurting yourself, you're going to need a professional to teach you how to get fit safely and effectively.

We're all creatures of habit: in what we do, what we eat, and how we spend money. There's a weight-loss company in Toronto that has a great tag-line that works for as well for your bottom line as it does for your waist line: "If you could do it alone, you'd have done it already."

I wish I'd said that, because I know it's true.

Your financial planning vehicle is running on cruise control. And the car is going to keep going at the same speed until somebody hits a different button.

Toll Roads & HOV Lanes

Toll roads and high-occupancy vehicle lanes (HOV) get us where we want to go faster. For them to work, we have to know what they do, the benefits they provide and the rules we must follow. And there are certain investment structures that can do the same for your savings.

Toll Roads

A toll road is a section of highway where a fee is assessed for passage. The primary advantage for travellers is that traffic is often lighter and you can get to your destination faster.

The RRSP and TFSA are like toll roads that can accelerate your savings. They are investment structures that allow you to save more effectively, such as an RRSP, a Tax Free Savings Account or a Registered Education Savings Plan. Each has its own unique features, but what they have in common is that they accelerate your investments to deliver a unique advantage so you can reach your goal faster. Knowing the rules for how they work is essential to leveraging the benefits.

Let's have a closer look at the three most important ones in Canada: the RRSP, the RRIF and the TFSA.

RRSP

The RRSP is the primary retirement program for most Canadians.

The core idea behind the RRSP is to put money away while you are working (and save tax at your top tax bracket), let it grow without any taxation slowing it down, and then withdraw from it during retirement, ideally at a lower rate of tax when you have stopped working and reduced your income.

Contributions are tax deductible from your regular income and the growth on the portfolio is tax deferred until you withdraw from the plan. Each working Canadian adult is provided with an annual contribution limit based on 18 percent of the income they earned the year before. Any amounts below the limit that have not been contributed annually can be carried forward to a future year.

The money you contribute has already been taxed by the time it reaches your hands. You receive a tax refund for the amount of tax you paid, so that the money deposited into the RRSP is effectively untaxed.

While the funds are in the plan, there is no taxation on the investment income or growth. You don't have to wait until retirement to access the funds in the RRSP, and the withdrawn amount is added to your annual income and subject to tax. There are also a few mechanisms available to loan yourself the money and not pay tax immediately if you use the funds to buy your first home or for education.

For many Canadians, the RRSP is their primary savings vehicle to fund their retirement.

RRIF

When you retire, you convert the RRSP into a Registered Retirement Income Fund (RRIF) and begin taking a regular income from it. You have to take out a minimum each year, but you can decide if you want to take more. It's like an RRSP in reverse. The income may be received annually, semi-annually, quarterly or monthly, it's your choice. Your RRSP can be converted to a RRIF at any age and it is mandatory to do so in the year your turn 71.

When the funds come out of the RRIF, the amount is added to your regular income for the year and you pay tax on it, just as if you were earning employment income.

Starting in the year after you establish a RRIF, you have to be paid a yearly minimum amount. The payout period under your RRIF is for your entire life. Your carrier calculates the minimum amount based on your age at the beginning of each year. However, you can elect to have the payment based on your spouse or common-law partner's age. You must select this option when filling out the original RRIF application form. Once you make this election, you cannot change it.

You can withdraw more, but not less than the minimum. The excess amount withdrawn cannot be applied as part of the minimum for the next year.

Earnings in the RRIF, like the RRSP, are tax-free and amounts paid out are taxable upon receipt.

You can have more than one RRIF, however I've found that having one RRIF is the most convenient option as you can hold a variety of different investments all within a single account for simplicity of administration. The rules that apply to self-directed RRIFs are generally the same as those for RRSPs.

TFSA

The Tax-Free Savings Account was created to work in concert with the RRSP, like the sidecar on a motorcycle. Like the RRSP, earnings growth and income is not taxed. However, unlike the RRSP, there is no tax deduction on contributions and also no future tax on withdrawals. Where the RRSP allows money to grow on a before-tax basis, the TFSA is designed to only tax the money once: when it's earned. The growth of the account is not taxed at all in the future.

Everyone over age eighteen in Canada has the same contribution amount, and it also carries forward if not used.

The TFSA is a wonderful structure for saving towards medium term goals and key milestones. It is also the primary savings vehicle for low and middle income earners, who would not see much of a tax saving by using the RRSP. Also, as future income is not taxed, there is no risk of losing any government benefits in retirement, such as the Guaranteed Income Supplement or having some of the Old Age Security payment clawed back.

The TFSA is a powerful addition to your planning toolbox. It's like a supercharger for your savings.

HOV Lanes

These are dedicated lanes that are available to vehicles carrying multiple occupants. They are designed to allow some lanes of traffic to flow more freely as there is less volume. If you're carrying more than one person, you can use the lane and go faster because there's less traffic ahead of you. Similarly, in a family's financial situation, if you have more than one person who can contribute to the journey, you're likely to get there faster.

First, they can help pay for gas, by contributing money to the journey. In most households, whether the partners manage their money separately or together, there is an ability to pool resources for a common cause. If you're all going the same way together then they can also help drive.

This isn't always the case. I regularly meet couples where one person does all the driving, meaning they are the dominant financial manager in the relationship. This is understandable, as most families have some delegation of labour, where one person takes care of these things and the other takes care of those things. But having an imbalance with respect to financial matters can be problematic. It's one thing if only one spouse can drive the car – the other one can always use Uber. But if only one spouse knows where the tax returns are, how the bills are paid with online banking and what their financial advisor looks like then they're very likely to have a problem.

> **The person who manages the money is also statistically the one who will die first.**

The good news is that this is an easy problem to address: I just teach the other spouse how to drive. It's essential that they become comfortable and able to drive alone managing the family's finances, in case one day they have to.

This was precisely the situation for Ralph and Mary Jane. When we met over 20 years ago, Ralph was a detective with a large metropolitan police force. Mary Jane was a registered practical nurse. They share a European background and have very traditional family roles. Ralph looked after the money and the outside of the house while Mary Jane looked after the kids and the inside of the house.

It didn't take long for me to point out that, as Ralph carried a gun at work, there was obviously an element of risk in his employment that most of us do not have. And with that risk came a heightened responsibility to have Mary Jane involved in the key financial affairs of the family. Ralph appreciated my concern and we began a campaign to involve Mary Jane in nearly all of our conversations. While reluctant and somewhat uninterested at first, Mary Jane is now a very active participant in the family's planning and is highly engaged in every element of their financial decisions. Ralph is very pleased, as Mary Jane feels more confident in their finances and, because they're making their most important decisions together, their marriage is stronger.

Roadside Assistance

There are a number of services available that will help you before your journey as well as while we're underway. The role of a great financial advisor combines the services of CAA, On-Star and sometimes a skilled mechanic.

CAA & On-Star

If you've ever set out on a long journey, then a quick stop at a CAA office before you leave can be time well invested. They have maps, customized route planners and many other services that will make your journey safer, more comfortable and less stressful. They'll give you advice based on helping hundreds of other people who have made the same trip. It's the same with financial planning: others have made similar journeys before you, and an experienced advisor has learned from guiding them. You're only going to educate your kids once, buy a vacation home once and retire once, for example. Advisors like me have done it hundreds of times. We will help you learn from other people's mistakes and successes and give you some perspective on planning your own way.

While CAA is great for helping you plan your trip, and can bring emergency assistance if you have a problem, many cars now come with satellite-enabled telematics that can help you in real time while you're on the move. They track you constantly and can provide advice and help as soon as it's needed.

I recently welcomed a new client to the practice who understood our value immediately based on a life-changing experience she had. Fiona had lost her husband and was learning to rebuild her life on her own. She had heard about the Camino de Santiago, which is an 800 km walk between France and Spain, ending at the Cathedral of Santiago de Compostela where the remains of St. James are said to be buried. It is a pilgrimage that has been followed since the Middle Ages and many take up this route as a retreat for their spiritual and mental growth.

Fiona decided, almost on a whim, to take the pilgrimage. She booked her ticket, and then went to a camping and hiking store to be fully outfitted for the trip. When she arrived, alone, she had no plan. She only had a rough idea of the route and had made no advance preparations. Indeed, she had no place to sleep the first night she arrived.

When I asked her why she hadn't done more planning, she said that if she had, she'd still be at home! "All my life, I've been a planner. And I've never really done anything", she said. "Sometimes you just have to go and figure it out on the way." True! And at least she had her gear.

Fortune seemed to smile on Fiona, and the day she arrived in France, she met Rafael, who was on his third pilgrimage to Santiago. She said he was invaluable in helping her on the journey. He knew the best routes to take, the best inns to stay in, when to take a break, what to eat and how to break her new boots in. They also developed a powerful, trusting relationship as they walked each step together. Fiona not only found a guide, she found a new friend.

When we were discussing the role we could play in planning Fiona's financial future, she said, "Oh, you're like Rafael! You're not just going to pack my back-pack; you're coming with me!"

Exactly. We advisors are like On-Star for financial planning.

The Mechanic

If you've ever been stuck on the side of the road, with the hood of your car up, staring at the engine compartment not knowing what you're looking at and feeling stranded and helpless, then you know the value of a great mechanic. Their job is to quickly assess and repair what is broken so you can get back on your journey with minimal interruption and stress. A great mechanic appreciates the complexity of the car's systems so that you don't have to.

I believe mechanics bring two key skills: they can fix a huge range of problems and they can also advise you on preventative maintenance so that you don't have many issues in the first place. For example, they can look at your tires and see if you're driving too fast or too aggressively. They can also see from your oil how well you take care of the car.

In a similar way, a great financial advisor can help fix things when there is a money accident. If you have too much debt, they can help with restructuring and budgeting. If you have been packaged out of a job, they can help you understand your entitlements and make a plan until you are back on track.

We'll cover more of these financial accidents a bit later.

With respect to financial maintenance, we can also see patterns of spending and other behaviour and, without judgment, bring those to your attention so that you can either adjust or plot a new course.

Life has movement, so your planning has movement. For example, if my car had performance tires that were rated for warmer weather, my mechanic might suggest I buy a set of winter tires so that I would be safer in the winter months.

My financial advisor may notice that I'm paying too much tax because I haven't structured my accounts and investments properly. A great advisor, like a skilled mechanic can find those opportunities and give you more mileage out of the plan you've already got.

Use Uber

So far, we've assumed that you'll be doing all of your own driving. You'll be responsible for finding your own maps, setting your own destinations, finding your own gas stations and changing your own tires. In the financial world, there are a lot of services available for people who want to manage all of their financial affairs by themselves. And there are also services that will help people who want assistance with some, but not all, of the work.

But just because you can, doesn't mean that you always should. I can walk into Home Depot, but that doesn't make me an expert contractor. Yes, I can change my own light bulbs and hang pictures, but I cannot (and should not!) renovate my own kitchen. Just watch one episode of Holmes on Homes and you can see the damage and cost of inexperience.

For many, hiring a professional to renovate their home is the right decision. Yes, there is a cost, but it's considerably less than doing it yourself and doing it wrong. The experts have the experience, the skill and the connections to do the job right the first time.

You've probably heard this old saying: *if you think hiring a professional is expensive, just wait until you hire an amateur!*

Before getting underway, the advisor works with you to understand your destination, your waypoints and the key milestones to visit along the way. They will add their insight and experience to make the journey faster and easier. They will also work to understand the style with which you want to get there. Do you want to go fast and take the highways, or do you prefer to go slower and take the side roads?

Once moving, the advisor is like having a GPS on the dashboard. He or she can tell you when to turn right and turn left, but you actually have to turn the wheel. If you choose to ignore them, it's your fault. Don't sue them if you drive off a bridge when they told you to go straight.

The next level of service is like calling Uber Black or a limousine. In financial planning and investing, it is also possible to hire a professional to do much of the work for you.

Along with advising you, some of the most skilled and experienced advisors, called portfolio managers, can actually do the driving for you. They have been given permission by the securities regulators and their firms to manage portfolios on a discretionary basis. The portfolio manager does not have to ask you when they need to change lanes or if they need to take a detour because there is an accident ahead or a shortcut is available. They're focused on getting you to your goal so you can sit back and enjoy the ride.

It's also comforting to know that you are in the hands of a professional who has advanced licensing, more experience and likely more skill than you have. In short, they're a better driver.

I've found that the people who are most interested and respond the best to discretionary management are those who've driven the hardest and longest on their own. They are usually my savviest clients, who have the most experience in managing their own portfolios. They appreciate the difficulty and respect the quality of work I do.

Amateur investors do not see the work, so they cannot understand the work, which means they do not appreciate the skill. When I fly in an airplane, I know there is a pilot. But as I'm not a pilot, I really have no idea how hard it is to fly a 747. But I do appreciate a smooth and stress-free flight.

Many people try to do too much themselves, in the belief that they are saving money. Sometimes, that is true. For low and medium skill tasks, you can often do the job yourself if you have the inclination, the time and are willing to make a few mistakes as you learn. For higher-skill tasks, the professional can often save you money, despite charging you an up-front cost.

We recently had our house renovated, and our contractor knew the best plumbers, electricians, painters and other trades and could hire them for a fraction of what they would charge me. That's because they know him and he brings them steady work. My friend did a renovation at the same time, and he had great difficulty just finding contractors who would do the work at a reasonable price. And he was certainly at a disadvantage in telling them apart.

My contractor can tell a great plumber from a lousy plumber. My buddy? How would he know until it was too late? To me, paying great people and getting great service is one the best ways to save money in the long run.

Two things that experience has taught me:

1. *Always pay up for quality*
2. *Cost isn't the same as price.*

Great financial advisors can do the same. They know all the toll roads, HOV lanes, short-cuts and rules of the road. They can help you maximize your RRSP, optimize your portfolio and lower your tax bill.

They can also perform feats of wonder. For example, in finance theory, risk and return are linked, so if you want more return, you have to take more risk. Keeping more of your money by saving tax is like earning a risk-free, guaranteed return. That's a magic trick, like pulling a bunny from a hat.

Advisors also fill a role in one's financial education that is sadly lacking in our school system. Since leaving high school, I've never had to conjugate a verb in French, dissect a frog or calculate a derivative. But I have had to balance my checking account, get a mortgage and make a will.

Advisors can help you find extra money in your budget, and they can tell you what investment products are worth paying for, and which ones aren't. They won't let you buy a cheap airbag. Indeed, one of their greatest benefits is helping you appreciate value if it's material to reducing your risk. I often see people neglect planning for when things go wrong, and that's how misfortune can turn to tragedy.

A few years ago I toured the BMW factory in Munich, Germany. During the tour, the tour guide mentioned that during the manufacturing process, BMW paints the brake pedal four times. Not once or twice. Four times. When I asked why, the guide replied, "Because we thought six was too much." I thought that was a strange answer. That was until I found out how their focus on over-engineering saved my life.

The following year I was driving in northern Ontario in my new BMW sedan, enjoying a beautiful spring afternoon. I came around a corner and there were two, yes two, full-grown moose in the middle of the road. They are massive animals, and there was no opportunity to go around them. I had to bring the car to a fast and complete stop. *Now.*

So, I slammed the brake pedal and the car went from over 100 km/h to 0 km/h in just a few meters. In a corner. Had I been in an almost any other car, I would have had a serious problem. The car may not have stopped and we would have hit the moose, or I may have missed the moose (mooses?), but I would have rolled the car or slid it into the trees on the side of the road as I lost control. However, because those German engineers decided to paint the brake pedal four times, and ensure the car was capable of higher performance than would ever reasonably be needed, I was safe. I appreciate that there were stability systems and braking systems in the car that did all the work so that I didn't have to.

The car stopped and I just stared at the moose. And they stared back. They wandered off and I drove away – a bit rattled, but completely safe.

A financial advisor can help you find a dollar, save a dollar and squeeze a dollar. And in rare cases, they can save you dollars when you least expect it. It's better to have more skill than you need right now, than need it and discover too late that you don't have it. Look for an advisor who cares about the paint on the brake pedal.

Modern Car, Classic or Dragster?

When you consider how you are going to fund your plans, and the help you might need to do so, you next need to think about how you're going to select the investment vehicles to use. Before you invest any money, you should have a solid framework for how you're going to select, diversify and manage those investments.

Modern Car

A modern car has outstanding performance, excellent fuel economy and the latest technological gadgets. It also has a combination of active and passive safety features that were unheard of just a few years ago. Along with air bags, seat belts and crumple zones, all of which protect you in a crash, they also have active systems that can help prevent an accident in the first place.

Similarly, a modern portfolio will have a combination of features, some visible and some under the hood, that if used properly can generate better results and with greater safety. Some of the features include:

$ Manager due diligence, search and selection

$ Diversification by industry, geography, asset class and investment style

$ Tax-aware investment product selection and trading, such as annual tax-loss harvesting

$ Disciplined portfolio rebalancing to maintain diversification and automatically sell-high and buy-low

$ Use of advanced investment structures and products, such as exchange traded funds, liquid alternatives and commodity pools, and

$ Regular performance reporting to track both individual securities and the portfolio as a whole against key benchmarks and risk budgets.

You do not need to know how fuel injection, anti-lock brakes and xenon headlights work in order to use them properly.

You do not need to be an engineer to drive. You just need to know how to use these technologies with a bit of skill and a bit of care.

A fully modern portfolio, just like a modern car, is both highly sophisticated and easy to use.

And so it is with a portfolio. You can easily access the latest investment strategies, mean variance optimization portfolio construction and risk mitigation techniques just by using some of the off-the-shelf investment services that are widely available at almost every financial institution and investment dealer. Many of these services are accessible to investors with as little as $1,000.

When used effectively, these innovations allow you to build portfolios that are safer, more robust, have greater effectiveness than you have ever had before. And they are complicated, just as new cars are complicated.

You wouldn't change the oil yourself on a new Mercedes, and you shouldn't tinker with the inner workings of a modern portfolio either.

Classic Car

While new technology makes things complicated, sometimes you just need a screwdriver. Many people like old, classic cars because they can change their own oil. Unlike a modern car, a classic is missing the safety features, advanced technology (sometimes no technology!) and conveniences. It is more of a raw experience, demanding much more skill of the driver and more regular maintenance and care. It can also be a lot more interesting! Yes, it may have drum brakes, manual roll-down windows and muscle-man steering but it may also look fabulous.

Consider a 1967 Jaguar E-Type or 1955 Chevrolet Bel-Air. They are beautiful machines that, with great care and enormous expense, make for a wonderful Sunday drive. But they have no seatbelts and break down regularly, so I wouldn't pack the family in them for a long road trip. Any boring minivan would be a better choice.

In the investment world, a classic portfolio would be one that is all about security selection and market timing. It would be investing like it's 1956, not 2016. The portfolio would have a lot of individual stocks and bonds and derive most of its returns from luck rather than skill. It would put a premium on things like fundamental research to try and find out information about a company that other investors didn't have. In this day of Twitter, Google and insider-trading charges, knowing more about a large business than someone else is close to impossible.

Classic portfolios will also pay attention to technical analysis, trying to predict the future from charts, graphs and other price movement patterns. While such work is fascinating in its complication and perceived sophistication, it's more illusion than reality. Most technical analysis has never been clinically proven to work.

While certain techniques and strategies may have their followers and true believers, it is closer to witchcraft and astrology than actual science. To an investment geek, few things have the siren call of moving averages, Fibonacci's and Bollinger Bands. But if you don't know what these are, you shouldn't play with them. Because, just like Odysseus, focusing on them can crash your portfolio on the rocks and leave you stranded.

Classic portfolios are best when treated like a second car that can be tinkered with by hobbyists. If you love changing your own tires, then go ahead and pick your own stocks. Just don't make the mistake of tinkering with your primary transportation.

Dragsters

A dragster or race-car can be either modern or classic. It can be a new, purpose built machine to conquer your local track or it can be a hot-rod muscle car from the fifties. In any form, it's built for speed, not comfort. I often see people building portfolios as though they're racing cars, particularly after several years of a bull market. They want them to be all high-octane, top fuel investments that will get them down the road as fast as possible, with their hair on fire and AC/DC rocking on the stereo. Risk be damned: I want to go FAST!

Very exciting. And when it breaks, blows up or slams into a wall, it will probably kill your financial plan. Leave the racing to the pros, or to a video game. There's no reset button in real life when you crash.

7

Staying on the Road

"Why aren't we flying?
Because getting there is half the fun."
– Clark Griswald (Chevy Chase)
National Lampoon's Vacation

There are number of things to keep in mind to be sure that you actually get to your destination comfortably, safely and reliably.

Check Your Mirrors

When you're driving, it's essential to watch where we're going. It's also essential to check your mirrors, do shoulder checks and keep an eye on the cars around you. Everyone has blind spots.

On a monthly basis, you should review your bank accounts and credit card statements. Here's a short list of what you're looking for:

$ How much am I spending?

$ What expenses were normal and expected? Which costs were unexpected?

$ Are there any mistakes or potential frauds?

$ What are my banking charges and interest costs? Are they reasonable?

Check Your Gas Gauge

As you review your spending, you need to review your savings each month too. Some of the key items to consider are:

$ Is my budget still working? Am I within the 10/70/20 budget framework? Should I adjust those guidelines?

$ Where can I reduce my spending and increase my savings?

$ Are my savings automated through payroll deductions or monthly bank transfers?

$ Do I have any extra lump sums that I can allocate to paying down debt or saving for my long-term goals?

Check Your Speedometer

Weather and traffic conditions can affect your speed when you're driving. You need to go slower when it's raining and when traffic is heavy. When you made your route calculations, you should have established some idea of how fast you need to drive, on average, to reach your goals.

Along with knowing your cash flow, you should also be keeping an eye on your investment performance. That performance measurement is like the speedometer for your money.

Each month, a cursory review of your portfolio statements is a good idea. Examine:

$ Did I make money?

$ What was up? What was down?

$ Were the markets up or down this month? Does my performance make sense based on what happened?

Every six months, additional analysis may be necessary, such as:

$ Am I going faster or slower than I need to go?

$ Do I need to change lanes and make a portfolio adjustment?

$ What do traffic patterns look like up ahead? Does it look clear ahead or might there be a detour coming?

Don't Ride the Brakes

While most investors are worried about going too fast and crashing the car, it's just as important to remember that you cannot go too slowly either. You're not going to get there if you keep the parking brake on. Overly conservative portfolios are just as dangerous as portfolios that are too risky. In both cases, you'll need far more money than you thought. If too risky, you'll keep losing money you didn't need to lose. If too conservative, the returns are too low and you'll have to save vastly more capital to generate the income you desire. If your money isn't working hard, then you'll have to.

Check The Oil

Regular maintenance is absolutely essential to keeping your car running safely and efficiently. If you don't stop once in a while to change the oil, rotate the tires and clean out the air filter, the car will not run well and you risk being stuck at the side of the road. Spending a bit of time and money on preventative maintenance actually makes for a faster time in the long run. Even Formula One cars need pit stops.

During the 6-month review process, you should lift the hood on your investment portfolio and see how things are doing. Is the balance still right? Anything leaking or broken? Everything working as it should? Are there any flat tires or underperforming investments that need to be changed because they are damaged? Or should I simply add more air (money) to them because they are temporarily low right now?

Also pay attention to the fact that, in a diversified portfolio, not everything should be 'on' all the time. If it is, then it's not diversified. If there is some investment that appears to be underperforming, then you may likely have the balance right. You don't run the air conditioning in the winter, but that doesn't mean you don't want to have it. You don't attach windshield wipers after it starts raining. The car and the portfolio both need to be properly installed so that they are ready when you need them.

Keep Adequate Insurance

You never know when bad things are going to happen. You could hit a patch of ice; a deer could run across the road or you could be T-boned by a texting driver. If you drive long enough, you're likely to have an accident. Hopefully it's a small one, and even those are expensive.

In your financial plans, you also need to plan for when things go wrong. Some costs you can self-insure, just like the deductible on your car insurance. But you also need to off-load risk to the insurance company in case something major happens. Misfortune can turn to tragedy if you don't have enough insurance to cover the big problems.

Some of the key risks that are so big we need to insure against them include:

$ Becoming disabled for six months or more

$ Being diagnosed with a critical illness or having a heart attack

$ Getting sick or hurt while out of the country

$ Dying and leaving our family with debt and without enough regular income to live on, or

$ Living a long retirement and needing extra care to manage day-to-day tasks, such as moving, washing or eating.

This is one area where receiving excellent professional advice is mandatory. You simply cannot make a prudent decision without a solid analysis of your requirements and making an honest assessment of the risks you face. You then require reliable and independent information on costs and insurance policy construction so that you buy as much as you need, but not more than you require. Insurance agents, like financial advisors, seem to be everywhere. And the great ones are hard to find. It's worth the search.

Rest stops

You can't drive all the way in one shift. You need to rest and sometimes you need to ask someone else to take a turn at the wheel. Drowsy drivers are just as dangerous as drunk drivers.

It's okay to take a vacation or enjoy a little luxury while on your way. You only get to drive on this highway once, so you need to enjoy the experience.

Driving too fast and too hard will break the car. And saving too hard and living too miserly can also be tiring. Taking a break with a timely holiday or a minor splurge on a luxury purchase can sometimes be the pause that you need to feel refreshed and motivated for the next leg of the journey.

Charles and Pamela

I recently had a meeting with Charles and Pamela. They have been extremely diligent savers, responsible investors and excellent clients to work with. Indeed, when we checked the mileage and speedometer on their plan, we discovered that they were well ahead of schedule on their way to retirement. Good news! We also discussed a European vacation they were planning for the next year. When I inquired about their budget, they already had everything priced out for an enjoyable three-star holiday.

I recommended that they go back to change all of their plans. Three-star wasn't going to cut it. They had worked hard, were ahead of plan and could easily afford a five-star luxury tour. We ran the math and informed them that they could spend twice what they were estimating. Fly business class and stay in finer hotels: that was my advice to them. Their financial plan was in great shape. Now they needed a better lifestyle plan to enjoy all of their hard work!

I gave very different advice to Nelly and Daniel. While both had reasonable careers in the public service, and had solid pensions to look forward to, they were spending more than they could afford on annual vacations. Their best friends had been more diligent in their younger years and had amassed a substantial nest egg that could fund their retirement. But Nelly and Daniel had not. So, they were burning through too much capital and cash flow trying to keep up with their friends. We amended their plan so that they could enjoy every other cruise, rather than every cruise that their friends took. And they had to enjoy the frugality of an interior stateroom vs. the luxury of a balcony suite. They could take some breaks but they needed to be shorter and less expensive than the ones they were taking.

Travelling with Children

As a parent, I know that children add new and wonderful complications to our lives. When travelling with kids, special considerations must be made.

First, you're going to go a bit slower and stop more often. The cost of raising and educating children will always be a compromise with your own retirement plans. It costs over $244,000 or $1,070 per month to raise a child to age eighteen in a middle-class Canadian home[3]. While everyone has different circumstances, I think this number is a great place to start when thinking about the financial impact of having children. Good thing we love them!

Along with saving for their education, they have regular annual expenses that go beyond just food and clothing. Sports teams, art, dance and music lessons, for example, can be very expensive. You also want to take time off and enjoy being with your children, so you often need to balance work and life commitments. I've yet to meet any senior executive who wishes they spent less time with their kids when they were younger. It's most often the reverse, and the regret of lost time can be heartbreaking.

On an annual basis, it's good practice to map out what these additional expenses will cost for the year ahead. Many parents underestimate these costs or forget to balance them against their own savings. Along with food and clothing, all of the children's activities need to be managed within the 70 percent lifestyle budget.

If you're finding that this isn't possible, then I'll humbly point out that your seven-year-old isn't likely to be the next Sidney Crosby and doesn't need the $600 hockey skates. Borrow a pair of hand-me-downs

[3] Retrieved October 2016 from http://www.moneysense.ca/save/financial-planning/the-real-cost-of-raising-a-child/

from an older sibling, cousin or the kid across the street. They'll outgrow them before the season is over anyway. If it's important, you'll figure it out.

Check The Map

Have you ever had the experience of driving along, and then forgetting where you were going? Sometimes the act of driving can become so routine, so mechanical, that you forget why you were doing it. And so it is with planning. You can get in a rut and lose sight of your destination and way points. It's like being stuck in traffic. You become so focused on the line of cars ahead of you that the destination becomes an afterthought.

When I have clients in for a review, I sometimes ask them to tell me again what they're planning for. What were the working assumptions they provided when we created the plan? In most cases, the destinations haven't changed. Yet often the waypoints have.

Am I still headed in the right direction? Is that where I still want to go?

To stay on course or perhaps plot a new one, it's important to check back to the key assumptions every once in a while.

Stay in Your Lane

The longer you invest, the more investment cycles you will see and the better prepared you are for change. You'll also learn not to change lanes too often. While it may appear that some lanes move faster, and some investments may temporarily be doing better than others, moving to capture that trend may put you in the wrong place.

If you've ever changed lanes to go faster, then you know what happens next: the lane you were in speeds up just as your new lane slows down. It's as though the universe punishes you for your impatience. This happens on the highway as well as in the supermarket.

Don't worry about what other drivers are doing and how fast they are going. Stay in your lane and stick to your plan.

Recalculating Your Route

Just as the GPS will recalculate a new route when issues arise on the original journey, you need to keep checking whether your path – and your driving – needs to adjust.

Drive Faster

If you're behind in your plan, you're going to have to drive faster to reach your destination in the same time frame.

Take The Highway

Highways move faster than city streets yet they can be much safer. Speed doesn't always equal risk. When investing, certain strategies work more consistently than others. For example, allocating to a well-managed portfolio of great companies that pay dividends is a proven strategy. Using a mutual fund or an ETF is the easiest and most effective way to do this. It's not as exciting as buying individual companies and following all the twists and turns of the market, but it will get you to where you want to go more reliably. Back roads are fun, but they are much slower.

This also means staying away from exotic investments that can look appealing but are probably more trouble than they are worth. Experimenting with hedge funds, emerging markets stocks and options strategies are best left to those who have time to make a mistake. All of these require considerable training and expertise to use properly. They can help, but their added benefits, in unskilled hands, do not outweigh their risk and complication. Incorporating them into a portfolio is like modifying your car; it might work but it may also void your warranty. Stay with what the engineers at the factory designed for the car. If you really want to add them, then hire an experienced portfolio manager to use them on your behalf.

Stop Less

Skipping a few waypoints and rest stops is another way to make up for lost time. Having a "staycation" instead of a Caribbean cruise, driving the old car for another year or eating at home rather than going out are all ways of economizing rather than splurging. Staying focused on the goal and sacrificing some of the waypoints is often necessary. Remember, waypoints are important, but some of them are luxury items. The destination is the key. If you're behind, then you can't afford to see all the sights. Prioritize.

Stop Sooner

If you just can't catch up, or you're not willing to sacrifice many waypoints, then you'll have to find a more suitable destination. It's not giving up on a dream, necessarily, it's modifying that dream to fit the reality of your situation. Maybe you'll have to find a way to live on less in retirement, or curtail some of the other plans you have made. Public golf courses instead of a private membership. Drive a Toyota instead of a Lexus. Find a new destination based on what is highly probable, not remotely possible.

8

Problems on the Road

"You can keep going and your legs might hurt for a week. Or you can quit and your mind will hurt for a lifetime."
– Mark Allen, Six-time Ironman World Champion

U sing my *Recalculating* process to get moving again is one thing. Indeed, you may have to do it several times on your journey. That's okay. When you're on the road you will likely have to deal with other problems as you go too. Surprise problems are part of life. The trick is knowing how to prepare for and react to them.

Back Seat Drivers

Back seat drivers are the outside influences that may be compelling and well meaning, but they are more likely to cause confusion. You've probably had the experience of driving down the road and being given unsolicited advice from other people in the car about how to drive, which lane to be in, shortcuts to take, go faster, go slower and so on. Some of it may be helpful, but most of it is distracting and dangerous. If you're not careful about how you filter and process this information, you might crash.

You will be confronted daily with an enormous number of outside influences that can easily disrupt, distract or destroy your regular plans. These influences can come from friends and family. They can come from media, blogging, tweeting, email, YouTube, Facebook, and all the other ways that information about saving, spending and investing can reach you. It seems like everyone has an opinion and technology allows all of them to be broadcast.

The trick is to figure out what to pay attention to and what to ignore.

There is a significant difference between information and wisdom.

The hardest voices to filter out are those that are closest to you. Your family, friends and co-workers are people you trust and care about. And they care about you, too. You believe they are well intentioned and, as they know you, they are in the best position to give you counsel. If you filter them too effectively, they can become frustrated that you are not listening to them.

It's best to take critical advice only from people who are trained and experienced to give it. Those who have no conflict, no bias other than what is best for you. If you had a sore stomach, your mother and WebMD may each have an opinion but if you are really in pain, see a doctor. It is precisely the same with money: seek out a well-qualified and proven financial advisor instead of listening to friends. And particularly those friends who like to follow the market. They are hobbyists and a little bit of knowledge can be a dangerous thing. You wouldn't trust your new car to a backyard mechanic, so don't take financial advice from amateurs.

Following Other Cars

It's easy to be a bit jealous of people driving in a faster cars or in a faster lane. This is the old 'keeping up with the Joneses'. Your friends may have a flashier car, take more vacations or have a nicer house, but so what? You don't know their whole story. You may see what they own, but you don't see what they owe.

Chasing Benchmarks

Instead of focusing on the rate of return needed to achieve or meet their goals, which is logical, most investors struggle to match the performance of some other benchmark, such as the S&P500 or Dow Jones. These indexes show the composite performance of a basket of stocks, and there is a specific rational for how each benchmark is created. It can be quite interesting to compare the performance of, say, a mutual fund to its relevant benchmark. However, neither is to be used as the sole criteria for assessing one's complete portfolio. They're best used like a weather gauge: if the benchmarks are up, then you should be up. If they are down, then you can expect to be down. If they're up by 8 percent and you're up by 7.5 percent, you have not underperformed. Unless your portfolio has taken the same risks as the benchmark, then it is not a simple apples-to-apples comparison. And yet, many investors assess the quality of their portfolios on the sole characteristic of whether or not they 'beat the market'.

$ *Beating the market* is **not** a financial goal.

$ *Retiring comfortably* is a financial goal.

$ *Sending my kids to college* is a financial goal.

$ *Paying off my mortgage* is a financial goal.

Successful investors have clear financial goals and mark their progress towards them. They focus on the destination. Lousy investors chase benchmarks and pay too much attention to what the other cars are doing.

The Dreaded Brother-In-Law Index

Trying to beat someone else's investment performance is perhaps the worst example of benchmark chasing. You probably have a friend, neighbour, co-worker, or brother-in-law who will generally brag or show off about the money they made in the stock market. Of course, you never see the money they lost or hear about the risks they took. Everybody's a winner in Vegas, right?

They may or may not be a more successful investor that you. All you know is that they love to toot their own horn. What's also true is that trying to beat them is a fool's errand.

What matters is how you progress towards *your* goal, with *your own* set of facts, opportunities and challenges. If your doctor told you to get your cholesterol to a certain range, comparing your cholesterol to Lance Armstrong's is a pointless exercise. Same with investment portfolios. The only portfolio that matters is yours.

Racing

Trying to race ahead and beat a benchmark is not a financial goal. Along with being the wrong focus, it is also a fruitless pursuit.

Dalbar, a financial services research firm, publishes a study that examines how investors actually do relative to key benchmarks. This report, called the Quantitative Analysis of Investor Behaviour, has been produced annually since 1994 and is widely read and respected. Dalbar compares not just what markets did, but what investors actually received. In the 2014 report, Dalbar reported that the S&P500 delivered 9.85 percent over the past twenty years. And that return was derived from doing exactly nothing. Simply holding the index over twenty years and allowing it to rebalance itself would have provided that return.

Now, one would reasonably expect that doing anything as an active investor should have improved on that return. If nothing got you 9 percent, then doing something, such as watching the business news, reading the business papers, listening to economists and strategists, talking with your stockbroker, whatever, should have given you a better return. If it didn't, then stop doing it.

What Dalbar found is that investors receive less than what the market delivered. The average investor did not receive 9.85 percent. They earned 5.19 percent.

Please allow me to repeat this.

Active investors underperform their own   investments.

Not just by a little bit either. They received about half of what their portfolio could have returned had they just left it alone. And this is not a singular event, limited to just this one study. Dalbar sees this same experience in every annual study they have done. The numbers may change a bit each year, but the degree of investor underperformance stays the same.

Why is this? Because investors are human! We make mistakes all the time! And investors make the same mistakes with great reliability and all of them are driven by the emotional challenges of investing.

One of the greatest emotional difficulties for investors is to ignore what the markets are doing and just let their investments be. Louis Rukeyser, the late host of Wall Street Week, had wonderful advice for investors in times of market stress. He said, *"Don't just do something: stand there!"*

If your portfolio is not doing well, maybe it's not your investments that are the problem.

Perhaps it's you. Slow down and let the portfolio work.

Weather

Just as weather can affect your travel plans, so too can market conditions. And like weather, you cannot change it – you just have to change *with* it.

There are essentially three kinds of markets you need to understand, appreciate and adapt to: bear markets, bull markets and market corrections. The first two types are like major weather systems; the latter is but a brief rain-shower.

Bear Markets

Bear markets are storms. They scare people. They are loud, cause damage and have lots of thunder and lightning. Fear of a bear market is what keeps most people either out of investing in stocks, or prevents them from investing well. Being afraid of them is like not wanting to drive in a blizzard or fog for fear of being in a multi-car pile-up.

The technical definition of a bear market is a 20 percent decline in the broad stock market. The S&P 500 is considered the best index to follow as it represents the largest 500 companies in the United States, ranked by size. So, the largest company is first, the second largest is second and so on. It's not a perfect benchmark but it is the one most often used.

Bear markets are common and a normal part of the investment cycle.

They are a weather pattern like a bad snow storm or a hurricane. There have been about thirteen bear markets since WWII. This translates into about one every five years. While this is their approximate frequency, it's essential to point out that their beginnings and endings are impossible to time, despite all efforts to do so.

The facts of bear markets are this: they come about roughly every five years, they destroy between 20 and 40 percent of one's capital, and then they are over in about two years. There is no avoiding them. They must be accepted, tolerated and endured.

Statistically inevitable, impossible to avoid (unless by luck), they are most dangerous for the emotional damage they inflict on investors.

No one likes to open their investment statements and see 20 percent of their money gone. Investors feel like victims, as if the universe somehow robbed them of their investment capital and jeopardized their most important financial goals.

For many people, their first experience with a bear market is also their last. Rather than developing the emotional maturity and financial discipline to remain invested through them, it is common to panic or act in anger and sell out, often right at the bottom of the market and at the worst possible time.

Experienced investors understand that bear markets are always temporary. They believe in an essential truth: advances are permanent and declines are temporary. And their faith in this sustains them.

Bear markets make everything cheap, sowing the seeds for the next bull market.

Markets go up <u>over all</u> of the time, just <u>not every</u> time.

Bull Markets

Bull markets are much more fun. Everything goes up.

Here are the facts for bull markets: they are more frequent and last twice as long as bear markets (bull markets average fifty-three months to twenty-five months for bear markets). Most importantly, the average bull market sees stocks rise over 150 percent.

The greatest risk with bull markets is missing them.

Most investors panic out of bear markets and miss the bulk of the next bull market. By the time they become convinced that things are better (and greed takes over from fear) most of the bull market is behind them and they dive right in at the end. More on this behaviour in a few moments.

Market Corrections

Consider market corrections like mini-bear markets. They are rainstorms, snowy days or heat waves. They are less severe, more frequent and every bit as frustrating.

Here are the facts on market corrections: they are moderate declines in stock markets and they happen at least annually.

Decline Amount	Historical Frequency	Normal # Per Year	Normal Recovery
10%	1 x year	1	8 months
5%	1 x quarter	4	2 to 3 months
3%	1 x month	11	2 to 6 weeks
2%	Often	18	Up to 4 weeks

Source: Standard & Poor's, FactSet, J.P. Morgan Asset Management. Returns are based on the price index only and do not include dividends. For illustrative purposes only. Analysis based on each type (size) of drawdown being independent. For example, the market does not typically see four 5 percent drawdowns and one 10 percent drawdown in the same year, but rather those 5 percent drawdowns may compound into a single 10 percent drawdown for the year. Data as of 1/31/15.

Indeed, the average annual intra-year decline for the S&P500 is about 15 percent. So it's completely normal to see your equity portfolio move by this much during any year.

The primary danger with market corrections is that investors will confuse them with bear markets and overreact. An emotionally charged decision to sell has historically been the wrong response, particularly because the time period to recovery is so brief.

It's critical to understand that your   portfolio, at the end of each month, will be down 41 percent of the time.

It's the other 59 percent you have to pay attention to.

Weather Forecasting

A great way to tell the kind of market we're in is to look at the current valuation. This is like understanding barometric pressure. A barometer won't perfectly predict the future, but it is helpful to know that conditions are changing. Understanding where we are and what's changing will help you prepare for what might be coming. If stock values are cheap, we're in a bear market and you should be buying while prices are low. If values are expensive, then be careful not to chase things as conditions could be about to change.

The way we interpret valuation is by looking at the price-to-earnings or P/E ratio. We take the stock price of a company and divide it by its annual earnings. If we had a company trading at $20/share and it generates $1 of earnings annually, then its P/E would be twenty. We can follow the same procedure for the market index as well, taking for example the S&P 500's level and dividing it by the total earnings of all the companies in the index. In this example, it would also be true that it would take twenty years of earnings, at this level, to buy one share of the index.

This is a simplistic way of determining valuation but it is also one that is commonly followed.

Valuations will vary considerably by industry. Companies that have little growth, like utilities, should have lower P/E ratios than high growth companies, like technology. This is because rapidly growing companies should see more earnings in the future and investors are willing to pay more for them. You need to be aware of what the normal P/E ratios are for particular industries so you can tell when they are overvalued or undervalued.

Historically, the S&P500 has an average P/E of around fifteen to seventeen. If we are seeing the P/E above seventeen, then we're nearing the end of the bull market and stocks are becoming expensive. Be careful. If the market's P/E is at twelve, then we're in the midst of a bear market and it is time to start buying while stocks are cheap.

History tells us that the most important thing to do in bull markets, bear markets and market corrections is NOT to react to them. Rather, it's best to plan for each, recognize them when they are here and then act accordingly. There are strategies to use in each environment, just like having the right set of tires for the season.

Install the Right Tires

If bear markets and bull markets are like seasons, then there are investments strategies that you should employ with greater success in each of them. Certain strategies work better in bull markets, some are more effective in bear markets and there a few techniques that work ideally in long side-ways market. Having the right investment strategy is like having the right tires.

Bull Markets = Performance Tires

In bull markets, the sun is shining and things are getting better all the time. The road may not be perfectly smooth, but it is certainly comfortable. As summer tires are designed to give maximum performance on dry roads, a portfolio that is focused on rising stock prices is the best choice. Commonly, using a broadly-based mutual fund or an exchange-traded fund (ETF) that holds growth stocks is the best-performing option. Companies that are growing their sales and revenues as the economy grows deliver the best returns. They tend to reinvest their earnings back into the company so they can grow even faster.

As an investor, most of your returns come from share prices going up. Shares become more valuable the longer you hold them. Diversifying into a number of growing industries and companies, and then holding on to them, is a winning strategy.

As most investors are late to recognize bull markets, I see the bulk of investors arrive just near the top of the market. All bull markets end with a blow-off phase. This is where investors are most optimistic and have the highest risk tolerance. They are investing aggressively, as many feel they missed the early part of the rally and now want to squeeze it for all they have.

It's critical to appreciate that markets are simply places where buyers and sellers meet to trade. If there are more buyers than sellers, markets go up. If more sellers than buyers, markets go down. When we reach the blow off phase, all the buyers are in. There are no more buyers. Everyone who has been chasing the market has now bought in. Guess what happens next? Remember, 70 percent of car accidents happen on sunny summer days[4]!

Bear Markets = Winter Tires

Markets go down. The storm is here. We now have vastly more sellers than buyers. Winter has come.

If you've ever driven on ice, then you know what it's like to invest in a bear market. You slip and slide as soon as you use the gas or brake pedal, and any sudden movement can put you right in the ditch. The key is to have lots of grip and make slow, steady progress.

Investing in a bear market means investing for income, not price changes. Stocks may be bouncing downwards, but look for companies that consistently pay a rising amount of income. In this environment, you want to invest like a landlord: look for income from your tenant, rather than trying to sell the building.

Companies that have very solid businesses, that work well even in lousy economic times, are usually solid bets. Owning things like banks, utilities, real estate companies and those that make the things we use every day (think toothpaste, food, fuel) are good choices. We're looking for stability, strength and reliability, not growth.

---

[4] Canada's National Collision Database, Transport Canada

The real trick is to earn dividends. Dividends are paid to shareholders as owners of the companies. In bear markets, the bulk of your return will come from dividends.

Here's a great example. From 2000 to 2010, the Dow Jones (a measure of thirty large U.S. companies that are felt to be representative of the U.S. economy) went exactly nowhere. Well, it bounced all over the place but it wound up at almost the same spot. The Dow hit 10,000 for the first time on March 29, 1999. I remember it as I was walking through the Scotia Plaza concourse in Toronto and people were cheering around a television set outside of the main Scotiabank branch. I remember walking past the same TV *(and it was EXACTLY the same TV!)* ten years later, as the Dow went through 10,000 again. There were no crowds this time to mark the occasion. In October 2009, the Dow finally climbed over the 10,000 once again. Permanently, it now seems. (It nears 20,000 as I write this.)

So, over ten years, the Dow went from 10,000 to 10,000. It bounced around like crazy but it turned out to be like Macbeth's despairing comment on life, "It is a tale, told by an idiot, full of sound and fury, signifying nothing."

Yet, buried among all the rubble of poor investment portfolios was one diamond: the dividends paid by the companies had doubled. At December 1999, the Dow Jones paid $146/share. Buy December 2009, it paid $297/share.

Just as snow tires give better traction on ice and let you move forward, dividends create a positive return even when markets seem to be going nowhere.

The other strategy that has the potential to work is to buy and sell as market volatility sends prices up and down. This is where active investment management will beat passive management. Here, having a great mutual fund manager or portfolio manager will be of greater advantage than just an index-focused ETF. You want people who see a fire sale when everyone else just sees a fire.

Finding these folks is tough and worth the effort, as you should not play the home game. Sitting at home trading your own portfolio is a recipe for disaster. You will not be smarter, trade faster or more economically than professional investors. Unless you're sitting on a trading floor, don't trade.

Have your financial advisor guide you carefully here. We're looking for investment companies and managers to handle the conditions coming up, not just those who did well in the past. We're looking for skill, not luck. You can't drive while looking only through the rear view mirror. Past performance is not indicative of future performance! Great people, strong processes and proven discipline are the critical factors as these *do* have performance persistence.

So, in bear markets, investing actively and harvesting dividends are the best strategies. Instead of focusing on your portfolio's value each month, look at how much income you collected. That will keep you on course.

Market Corrections = All Season Tires

Most of the time, markets are between the extreme overvaluations of bull markets and the deep corrections of bear markets. They move mostly up and down, but higher over the long term. A good visual is to imagine yourself walking up a flight of stairs with a yo-yo. Your portfolio will bounce daily like the yo-yo, and the upward movement over time is the long-term trend of the market. Be the stairs, not the yo-yo.

Most of the time you need to invest in a balanced way, so you're not caught off guard by extreme markets. Back to our driving metaphor: all season tires are not necessarily the best in every condition, but they have enough flexibility that they are really good in most conditions.

They have a good balance of compromises: decent on wet roads, quiet on dry roads and they can handle light snow.

And so it is with a portfolio: it should be a balance of compromises. It should deliver some growth, generate a bit of regular income and have some safety. It should be intelligently diversified and risks should be spread out. It should be boring and taste like vanilla ice cream. If you are getting solid and boring returns, then it is doing its job. Your challenge will be in not screwing it up and trying it to overdrive it.

I should point out that professional investment advisors and portfolio managers get nervous and worried at exactly the time when our clients are the happiest. We're also the most greedy, eager and excited when they are the most terrified. It's because we recognize these patterns and have learned to use them to our advantage, rather than being abused by them.

Every driving instructor will tell you to practice defensive driving. In the same way, great money managers understand that great investing means being cautiously optimistic.

Investing should be as exciting as farming. Boring works.

Roadblocks, Traffic Jams & Detours

These unexpected financial challenges will appear directly ahead of you and slow you down. Their common feature is that they were caused by someone else's financial accident. You didn't crash, someone else did. It was their problem but you're going to have to deal with it as it affects your journey.

The roadblock could be caused by losing a job, not getting a pay raise or your company going on strike, for example. Perhaps you got sick and couldn't work.

Whatever the cause, you are now delayed on your trip and you have to determine if the situation is a temporary slowdown or if the road is permanently blocked. If temporary, then maybe you just have to wait for traffic to clear and keep focused on your destination. Maybe that bonus will come a few months from now or the strike will be over soon. You just have to hang in, sit tight and wait.

But if the situation has changed more significantly and you need to find a detour, then it's time to run the Recalculating process, starting with *Where Am I?* as described in chapter two.

Mark and Laura

Several years ago I began working with Mark and Laura. Mark had worked for most of his career with a major corporation that was closing down its operations in Canada.

As part of his severance package, he was given job counselling to find a new occupation. His previous job was very specialized and his skill set had become extremely narrow. Finding a similar job at another company was simply not an option. He was too young to fully retire, and his pension would not have supported the family anyway. He had hit a significant roadblock. And he also found himself stuck in a traffic jam as many people with his employment background were on the job market at the same time.

He discovered in his career counselling that his personality traits and his experience with coaching amateur sports made him well suited to working with other people. He began an entirely new career in social services as a personal support worker. Today, he is much happier in his new role than he ever was at the old company. Through hard work and courage to try something new, Mark has turned his roadblock into a wonderful new journey.

Not all detours present themselves as initially negative.

There could be a positive surprise that changes our course. Maybe your child was accepted into a great school and it will cost you more than you expected.

A few years ago, my niece got married – and decided to do so on a beach in the Dominican Republic. Everyone in the family who wanted to go had to pay their own way. We weren't going to miss it, so I flew my wife and two kids to a beautiful resort for the week. We had to change our annual vacation plans and adjust our budget to make it happen, and so we did. Happily!

One of the major roadblocks I suspect most baby boomers will encounter is that their parent's retirement will affect their retirement. We discussed this earlier when we considered helping hitchhikers and stranded motorists.

As people today live longer, meaningful lives, and they are vital into their eighties and nineties, they are still alive when their children retire. It will be a very common occurrence for people to be entering retirement, and find themselves being very directly involved with their parent's care. They may have to contribute more financially and emotionally than they had expected when they planned their own retirement.

Simultaneously, their children are living at home longer, delaying careers and their own family formation. The baby boomers have been nicknamed the sandwich generation as they are stuck between helping both their elderly parents and adult children at the same time.

Speeding Tickets, Tolls & Fees

Having to pay extra costs for speeding tickets, tolls and fees are all realities of driving. There are similar costs that are the realities of dealing with money. Appreciating what they are and how they affect you is important if you want to deal with them properly.

Taxation

Taxation is the first major cost you encounter with money.

While taxes are inevitable and necessary to run our country, it is also your responsibility to minimize them as much as possible. Normally, we all accept that risk and return are linked together. To earn more money, you would have to take more risk. Yet, if you can reduce tax and keep more of what you earned, whether it's through working or investing, it is like earning an extra return. And it is with no added risk. This is a magic trick worth knowing.

> **Taxes will be part of every financial decision you ever make.**

Being tax aware is like being a defensive driver. Knowing how to manage taxes is like knowing the rules of the road. Taxes are the rules of the road for money. Remember, it's not what you earn, it's what you keep!

There are three key strategies for minimizing taxes: deduct, defer and divide.

Deduct

A deduction is a claim to reduce your taxable income. A deduction will reduce your tax bill by an equal amount to your marginal tax rate. Some common deductions include:

$ Pension plan contributions

$ RRSP contributions

$ Safety deposit box fees

$ Interest expense

$ Union/professional dues

$ Alimony/maintenance payments

$ Employment expenses

$ Moving expenses

$ Professional fees, and

$ Child care expenses.

Note that your ability to use any deductions is based on your individual personal and family situation. Deductions also change frequently, in their availability, amount and applicability.

The best way to ensure you are maximizing all of your deductions is to have a professional accountant prepare your taxes or at least review them periodically. They should be up to date on all of the current deductions that are available to you and how to use them effectively.

If you wish to do your own tax return, be sure to read the tax guide fully, so you are aware of the major deductions you can claim.

It's also helpful to use a good tax preparation software program that can guide you through key deductions. Some of these programs will also run a check of your tax return to see if you've filed for the deductions properly and completely. Finding just one deduction that you may have otherwise missed can easily be worth the cost of the program.

Defer

The next method is to defer or delay paying tax for as long as possible. A deferral strategy is to delay tax payments into future years.

Deferring tax means you might eliminate the tax this year but you will eventually have to pay the tax down the road.

Inflation means future dollars are worth less than today's dollars.

If you can pay your tax bill, say, five years from now, it will be with dollars that are actually worth less than today's dollars.

I'm not saying that you shouldn't pay your taxes on time. You must, or you're going to incur penalties and interest costs. The trick is to push them as far into the future as reasonably as possible.

For example, let's say you are entitled to a bonus at work. If you receive the bonus before December 31, it will be taxable in the current year. However, if your employer will pay it to you on January 2nd of the following year, then you have an extra year to deal with the taxes.

In a similar way, when you look at investments, some of them pay income annually. A bond, for example, usually pays interest twice a year. That interest is taxable to you in the year you receive it. Dividends from stocks are also taxed in the year you receive them.

There is a third kind of investment income that is taxed very differently: capital gains. Capital gains are basically profit. If you buy something for $10 and sell it for $30, then you have a profit, or a capital gain, of $20. In most jurisdictions, you pay the lowest rate of tax on capital gains vs. interest or dividends. Along with the lower rate of tax, note that you only trigger the capital gain when you sell the investment. It is not taxed every year. This means that you could hold an investment for many years and you'll only pay tax when you sell it.

One of the reasons that great investors take their time and buy quality investments is that they want to hold them for as long as possible to maximize the deferral of taxes. Instead of paying taxes each year on a bond, you could hold a share of a great company, like McDonalds or Apple, for many years and pay no tax on their growth while you hold it. If those stocks pay a dividend, then you'll pay tax on the dividend income but not on the increasing value of the shares.

Earning capital gains is a vital part of any long-term investment portfolio. With a patient and conservative strategy, you can defer paying taxes on your holdings and thus watch them grow faster than if they were taxed every year.

Divide

Dividing taxes is the ability to take an income and spread it among a number of different taxpayers. These techniques are often called income splitting.

For example, one person with annual income of $70,000 will pay more income tax than two people ((say husband and wife) each paying tax on $35,000. As our tax system is progressive, it means that as you earn more income you will pay a higher rate of tax. There are key tax brackets which are the divisions at which tax rates change. Income past a certain point will be taxed at a higher rate.

Because we are taxed as individuals, knowing how to spread taxable income across family members properly can lower the family's overall tax bill.

You cannot arbitrarily decide who is going to claim what amounts for income.

There are strategies to divide income within the tax rules, such as:

$ Spousal RRSPs help split income in retirement.

$ Splitting Canada Pension Plan retirement benefits with your spouse.

$ Pension splitting for retired couples.

$ Investing non-RRSP savings in the lower income family members.

$ Utilizing RESP contributions.

$ Payment of wages to family members (through a business).

$ Use of partnerships or corporations to earn business income.

$ Utilizing either inter-vivo or testamentary trusts.

The use of these strategies is best decided on after a conversation with your tax professional and a great financial advisor. The key is knowing how to use these techniques properly and effectively.

Investment expenses

When you buy a car, you pay attention to the overall operating expenses required to keep and use it. This is more than just the sticker price on the window. Similarly, investing is not free, so you must be aware of the costs you incur when putting your money to work. And just like with a car, cost isn't just price!

While all cars may have four wheels, doors and a steering wheel, not everyone wants to drive a Honda and not everyone can afford a Ferrari. They share many characteristics, but different buyers will place value on different qualities. Some will value luxury over thriftiness, safety over speed, the latest technology over basic transportation.

The key point is that cheap does not automatically equal good.

The car you drive is a reflection of your financial circumstance and the combination of values you carry towards vehicles. Cost is just one variable among many.

When investing, you must identify both the price of your investments and compare that to the quality and value of the services you receive. In a moment I'll identify some of the main investment expenses you can expect to encounter and provide a framework for assessing them. Again, there is no right answer for all investors.

What I can share with you is that your success as an investor is not tied to the cost of the investment, despite what the press may tell you.

No, what you DO with the investment is vastly more important than what you paid for it. Your actions, and the advice you receive to buy, sell, or hold are materially more important than any fees you pay.

With that in mind, there are two key types of investment expenses you should be aware of.

Transparent Expenses

Transparent expenses are costs you can see and that you pay for directly. Some examples would be:

$ An annual account or administration fee

$ A trading commission to buy or sell a stock, or

$ The annual fee you pay your portfolio manager or financial advisor, often stated as a percentage of your managed assets.

You will see these costs reported on your regular statements in the *activity* or *transaction history* section as they are incurred. In many cases, you may also receive an annual statement that highlights these costs. Some of them may be tax-deductible.

Embedded expenses

Embedded expenses are bundled into the investment products you buy and can take many forms.

One of the most common embedded expenses is the management fee that is part of every mutual fund and exchanged-traded fund. These fees pay for the management, operation and marketing of the funds. As the costs are shared amongst all investors in the fund, they are billed to the portfolio. The cost to directly bill investors would be prohibitive. Your performance is reported net of these expenses.

You may also see the term MER, which stands for Management Fee Ratio, which is the total amount of fees, including tax paid, and divided by the size of the fund. So, if you see an MER of 1.05 percent, it means that your fund has incurred a total of 1.05 percent in costs and this is deducted from your portfolio. Your performance will be reported net of this cost.

Sales commissions are another type of embedded expense that are baked into the purchases and sales of many mutual funds: front-end loads, back-end loads and trailing commissions.

A front-end load is applied so that the commission is taken from your initial investment. If there is a 2 percent front end load and you invest $10,000, then $200 is paid as a commission and your net investment is $9,800.

When a back-end load (also called a deferred sales charge, or DSC), then all of your money is put to work immediately. You do not pay a direct sales commission. Instead, the mutual fund company will pay your advisor or dealer a commission. The catch is if you sell before a defined period of time then you will pay a penalty to exit the fund. This penalty might be as much as 5 percent of your withdrawal in the first few years, and then declining to 0 percent over as long as seven years.

When you buy a mutual fund, your advisor should offer you the choice of a front-end load or a back-end load. If you're planning to keep the investment for a long time, then perhaps the back-end load may appear as the best choice.

However, many marriages do not last seven years and the costs for exiting the investment, if circumstances change, can be significant. Also, the advisor or dealer is paid as much as 5 percent of your initial investment when you select the back-end load option.

The industry is moving to reduce or eliminate the back-end load option as it has been the subject of many investor complaints over the years. So, consider this fact if they recommend that option to you.

In either case, whether a front-end load or a back-end load is used, most funds will also pay your advisor or dealer an on-going commission, called a trailing commission, or a trailer, for servicing your account over time. This may be as much as 1 percent per year and is added to the MER of the fund you hold.

It's important to note that the trend in financial services globally is towards greater transparency in fees so that investors are fully aware of the costs associated with the products and services they buy. Increasingly, advisors and their dealers are putting a focus on transparent vs. embedded costs structures.

Almost all mutual funds are now available with an F-class or fee-based class that removes the trailing commission from the fund and allows your advisor to bill you directly.

This has the advantage of removing any potential conflict from the product as you are paying your advisor rather than the fund company so they receive no compensation for choosing one fund over another.

As an investor, you should know all the costs you incur so you can evaluate the services you receive from your financial institution and financial advisor properly.

Again, cheap is not automatically the best.

Just ask anyone who's hired a cheap contractor to work on their house.

Great financial advisors, financial planners, and portfolio managers are rare and in demand. They charge for their professional advice and astute, experienced investors pay it with the full appreciation that the benefits of a disciplined process, up-to-date investment and tax knowledge and outstanding customer service are worth more than they will ever pay.

In all cases, there is a value in paying up for quality. Never buy cheap light bulbs unless you like climbing ladders in the dark.

What is the right price?

Keeping your costs to a reasonable level is a key part of investing. If your car manufacturer says the vehicle will run fine on regular gas, then there is really no point in paying 30 percent more for premium gas. Similarly, putting cheap fuel into your Porsche is a terrible idea.

If you have paid for a high performance car, then feed it the best juice you can.

DIY

If you are doing all of your own investing, then you should keep your costs to a minimum. If you're doing most of the work yourself, then it makes sense to pay only for the products you use.

Use a discount broker to buy your stocks and ETF's. Many discount brokers and banks will not sell you F-class mutual funds, as these are for fee-based advisors. Avoid buying regular mutual funds in a discount account as there's no point in paying for a 1 percent trailing commission if you're not getting on-going advice.

Trading is not investing. I saw an ad recently for one of the major on-line brokerage firms that is offering 300 free trades if you open an account with them and deposit at least $100,000. Three hundred free trades! And they even have an app so you can trade from your iWatch!

This is insanity. If you trade 300 times in a *decade* on a $100,000 portfolio, then you're trading too much. And if you need to trade your portfolio from your iWatch, then you have a more serious problem. Get some friends, a hobby or a dog. Anything that resembles a real life.

A portfolio is like a bar of soap: the more you touch it, the smaller it gets!

Trading is not free. Even if the transaction commissions to buy and sell are kept low, there are also bid and ask spreads that eat into the value of your portfolio. Many people are not aware that there are actually two prices whenever you trade a stock: the *ask* price, which is what the seller wants to collect, and the *bid* price which is what the seller is willing to pay. They are never the same.

In the case of a widely traded stock, like General Electric or Microsoft, these prices are perhaps less than a penny apart. In a rarely traded stock, they could be several pennies apart. If you do a lot of transactions, you'll usually be selling at the bid and buying at the ask. The difference could eat into a lot of your capital.

Further, if you are trading outside of a registered account, like an RRSP, then you will have to keep track of any capital gains and losses on each individual trade. Not only will this have a higher administrative burden, you will lose one of the most valuable benefits of investing in stocks: long term capital gains tax deferral. If you just held the stock of a great company for years, rather than trading in and out of it, you will push off any tax bills until years into the future.

Remember, great investing is the precise opposite of trading. As my Granny taught me, *you don't dig up the carrots to see how they're growing*.

I have had many DIY investors come to me after they are tired of running their own portfolios. The stress of managing the positions and staying on top of the portfolio was an additional cost that they no longer wished to bear. And in almost every case, when I reviewed the portfolio, I noticed that the bulk of their returns, if they had any, almost always came from just a few stocks. And those were also the stocks they had held over time. In every case, they were high quality, blue chip, dividend-paying stocks that they never traded. They knew that these were the bedrock of their account. Yet, instead of building on that foundation and simply tending the garden, they put countless hours of time into trading other stocks that just came and went. Rarely would these positions bear fruit.

I liken this position to the junk drawer you have in your kitchen. I'm sure you have one – we all do. It's where we keep extra AA batteries, coupons for the pizza place, paper clips, the business card for the guy who came door to door offering to paint the house and we said we'd get back to him, all that debris of daily life that we don't want to throw out but we just have nowhere else to put it.

A few years ago, we decided to renovate our house (yes, I hired a professional!) The renovation was extensive so we decided to move out of the house for six months rather than live through dust and disruption. One of the tasks my wife gave me was packing up the junk drawer in the kitchen. When I approached the task, I felt a bit overwhelmed. Where do I start? What do I throw out? I knew that most of it was junk, but what if there was something in there I might need?

As we were moving into the rental apartment, my wife asked me why the old kitchen drawer was in the new dining room. I figured that rather than sort through it, it was easier to just take it with us! I had pulled the drawer out of the old kitchen cabinet and brought it over, completely undisturbed, into the new apartment. I carried it like a newborn baby. That seemed like the easiest and most practical solution to me.

Later, my wife unpacked the old junk drawer. Almost all of it went into the trash. What remained were five paperclips, three batteries, a note pad and one working pen. All the coupons had expired and she didn't like the painter guy anyway.

The lesson is that sometimes you just have to get serious and throw out the junk. And that my wife is a very wise person. ☺

The bottom line is that if you're going to manage your own money, then paying attention to costs matters. And that includes paying attention to your own time and ability. There is a cost to the hours you will need to spend managing your own portfolio, and a price that will be paid if you are less than great at it.

Hiring an Advisor
Whether they are called financial planners, investment advisors, portfolio managers, financial advisors, or wealth managers and despite the fact that some of their capabilities may differ, at their core all offer some level of financial advice to investors for a fee or commission.

Before seeking out an advisor, or perhaps thinking about the one you currently have, you should have a clear idea of what kind of support and service you are looking for.

Some investors are looking for a person who can help them with their portfolio construction and give them good ideas from time to time. The advisor may also be a sounding board for the investor's ideas and sometimes play devil's advocate. The types of investments used may include mutual funds, stocks, bonds, term deposits, ETF's, hedge funds and any other securities the advisor is licensed to offer to clients. In many cases, the advisor also has access to extensive research into financial markets, economic reports and investment analysis that they can deliver to their clients to help in decision making.

This type of relationship is called *non-discretionary* as the investor makes all of the investment decisions based on input and advice from the advisor. The advisor completes the transactions according to the investor's instructions.

At no time may the advisor make a buy or sell decision without explicit permission of the client. This includes other elements, such as the price at which the security was transacted, when the transaction took place or the quantity purchased. The investor may give some limited discretion, such as "buy 500 shares of IBM at $50 or better". This would be a day order and if the advisor has not been able to buy IBM for $50 or less by the end of the trading day, then the order is cancelled. The investor may also give some discretion in terms of time, such as leaving the order open for thirty days. In any event, the nature of this relationship is that the investor retains full control over all investment decisions. The client is driving the car and the advisor is like the traffic reporter on the radio, giving information and counsel that the driver can either act on or ignore.

Some investors desire a higher level of service and will seek out a *discretionary* advisor, called a portfolio manager. Earlier I referred to this as hiring Uber: you provide the destination, arrange for a desirable course and give some rules on how they are to drive. After that, you can sit back and relax while they take care of all the details and administrative tasks involved in managing your money. If a security is to be bought or sold, then the portfolio manager will make those individual decisions as they fit into your overall strategy.

There are a few key considerations when deciding to hire a portfolio manager. The first is that they are generally among the most experienced, educated and trained investment professionals in the financial industry. Second, unlike an advisor, the portfolio manager acts in a fiduciary capacity, which means that they have a greater duty of care to the investor. This is a higher legal standard that requires them to put the investors' interests ahead of their own. Doctors and lawyers also operate to a fiduciary standard.

As part of the process, the portfolio manager will work with you to create an investment policy statement that outlines your goals, your time horizon, liquidity needs and other important factors that will influence how they manage your portfolio.

With respect to how you pay them, advisors can charge a commission for each transaction or an annual fee for managing your accounts. Portfolio managers, on the other hand, can only charge a fee based on the value of your portfolio. This is so that they never have a conflict of interest in that they are not paid by any of the products they choose for you. Only the investor can pay them.

Most portfolio managers will have a higher minimum account size or portfolio value before they will engage with a client. And, as they have a higher legal standard and deliver a high level of client service, they may also have a marginally higher cost than a non-discretionary advisor.

Planning services can be offered by either a discretionary portfolio manager or non-discretionary financial/investment advisor. Helping you in identifying your key goals, balancing compromises among them and building savings and investment strategies to achieve them is a core skill that will have tremendous impact on your ultimate success as an investor. A great planner can help you navigate complex tax rules, insurance products, estate planning and other matters in a cohesive manner. Some may charge for this service independently and some will include it in their annual fee rate.

Many advisors will offer financial planning as a one-time event, to be completed at the beginning of the relationship. In my view, financial planning is becoming the free toaster of the investment business. In most cases, the plan is simply a retirement income projection. While helpful, it is usually out of date as soon as it is finished printing.

Financial planning is not about creating a plan. Rather, it is a process of balancing competing financial goals against the limits of financial capital and time. Life has movement, markets have movement, goals have movement, and so must your plan. A great financial planner is like a terrific quarterback: they have a game plan when they start the game, but the trick is how they adapt and call audibles on the field.

It is normal that an advisor or portfolio manager who charges based on your portfolio will cost between 1-2 percent annually for the services they provide. They commonly have fee tiers, so that as you invest more with them, the fee rate declines. In some cases, their fee may be tax-deductible for you. This cost will be in addition to any embedded fees inside the products, such as mutual funds or ETF's, that they purchase for you. Again, if they use these products, they should be using the "F-class" versions that have no trailing commissions built into the management fees.

Should you pay for an advisor or portfolio manager? And what is the best way to pay them? By commission per trade or on an annual fee?

While everyone may have their own view of this, my experience in renovating our house gave me an interesting perspective.

We worked primarily with two professionals: an interior designer and a general contractor. Both were fantastic. And yet the way they billed us for their services left a very different impression for me when we were done.

Our designer, Gabrielle, billed us by the hour. While she had a great vision and we're happy with the style of our home, I was unhappy every time I received a bill from her. I never knew if we were really getting all of the time she was billing me for. Did it really take three hours to source those pillows? Five hours to shop for curtains? And when were we done? When would the bills actually stop? We never had a ceiling on the total cost for the project so I was never sure when we would reach the end. It seemed like she would keep billing as long as we kept talking to her. The open-ended-ness of the relationship made me uncomfortable.

Our general contractor, Dan, had a completely different approach. Once we discussed in detail the scope of the project, he gave me one price for the entire job. A reasonable number of changes and adjustments were included in that price. If we requested a change later that was more expensive than originally anticipated, he quoted me on the additional amount.

So, while we had less transparency into his charges (I still have no idea what my new kitchen cabinets cost, for example), I was much happier knowing in advance what the project was going to cost me. There were no surprises. Did I pay too much? Could I have negotiated with his trades separately to get a better deal? Maybe, but I doubt it. He knew which plumbers, dry-wallers, electricians and other trades to hire. They were always on time and worked efficiently.

Not only did Dan know which trades were best, they also worked diligently for him, as he represented a steady flow of work for them, whereas my house would only be one job. Moreover, Dan and his crew have built many houses, so they have great skill. You only retire once, so it pays to consider the value of hiring a professional advisor who has done it hundreds of times.

Looking back, while Gabrielle gave me full transparency into her prices and process, I felt more comfortable and had greater certainty with Dan's approach. Both are right. Dan's style was right for me.

Hang on to the Wheel!

Once you feel that you are financially off course, it's very easy to give in to the feeling of lost control. That emotional response, that feeling of helplessness is understandable. And also the most dangerous and damaging thing you can do. If your car went into a skid, you should try and steer your way out of it. Letting go of the wheel and closing your eyes will not avert the crash. Only positive, intelligent action can save you.

So, once you know you have a problem, the most important next step is to take emotional control of it, recognizing you have the power to change the outcome. And making no changes is also a decision. Either way, you have to own it.

Steer into The Skid

The direction out of your problem is connected to the thing that caused the problem. If you're spending too much, then the solution is to focus on your spending habits. If you're saving too little, then you'll have to focus on techniques to save more. If you're taking too much risk in your investments and your portfolio is a mess, then you'll have to learn to become a better investor. If your job doesn't pay you enough and is a dead end, then you'll have to figure out how to improve your skills and get a better job. The solution lies within the problem. Steer into the skid!

Keep Everyone in the Car

If your passengers also feel like they're lost, then they may start blaming the driver. They may want to drive the car themselves or just get out and start walking. Some will look for another car. None of these options are ideal. Blame is not helpful. Instead, be in the moment and understand that only a rational, logical plan can fix the problem. Shouting and hurt feelings, while entirely understandable, are not going to make things better. No one ever shouted their way out of a crash. Blame is paralysis and we need to keep moving.

The key is understanding what happened to take you off course and then moving on to fixing it. And most importantly, paying attention, so that you do not repeat the same mistake in the future.

9

Preventative Maintenance

Nothing Works Every Time.

But Some Things Work Over All The Time.

-   *Darren Coleman*

There is no security or investment strategy that will produce strong, positive results every day, every month or every year. Everything has risk.

But some things have proven to work over long periods of time. They are reliable and have the best long-term outcomes. There are three core elements that are actually easy to identify:

1. Invest for dividends.

2. Stick with quality.

3. Diversify and stay in the middle of the road.

Fight The Right Dragon

I am regularly amazed at how people are afraid of the wrong things. I mentioned earlier the nervous smoker outside the airport, more afraid of a plane crash than getting cancer. Statistically, the safest place for her is inside the aircraft where she can't smoke.

Similarly, I find many people are nervous about investing in stocks. They have a fear of the stock market that keeps them from owning some of the best companies in Canada, the United States and around the world.

They are not afraid of great companies – they are afraid of market volatility. Watching your investment go up and down, making and losing money on paper every day is frazzling. I get it.

What you should be afraid of is the thing that happens every day that you don't see: inflation. Every year, your lifestyle costs more than it did last year. Relentlessly. And not only are the things you buy getting more expensive all the time, there are new things to spend your money on that didn't exist a generation or even a few years ago. What was your monthly internet bill in 1990? How much did you spend on Netflix in 2005? iTunes? What will you spend in 2025, for example, on a technology hasn't been invented yet?

Your biggest financial risk is not the market. It's your credit card.

Invest for preserving *income*, not capital.

Don't worry about protecting a dollar. Worry about protecting what a dollar *buys*.

Do Regular Maintenance

Portfolio reviews are like changing your oil. You don't need to do it every day, but you should do so a few times a year.

Review your wills and power of attorney documents every three to five years and again if family conditions change. Rules and laws change too. For example, does your will specifically grant someone else the power to access your social media and other online accounts? Recent cases suggest that this is now necessary. And consider how much of your professional, social and financial details are now only accessible online through a password-protected device or network. How much of your life is kept on your phone?

Know Your Target Speed

You have to drive fast enough to get there, but not so fast that you crash. Speed itself doesn't kill and highways are the safest roads. Going too slowly and taking side roads may take too long. What's really dangerous are speed differentials: going too fast on back roads and too slowly on highways.

Once you've mapped out your destinations and waypoints, you should know the average rate of return you need to realize to achieve your goals. Along with that, you should also have an acceptable range of return that coincides with the portfolio. For example, if you're aiming for 6 percent annually and you have a balanced portfolio then you should also expect the normal range of returns to be +/-12 percent. That means if everything went your way, the fastest the portfolio can grow is 18 percent in one year. Highly unlikely, but that would be its top speed. It can't go faster than that because, like a Volvo, extra airbags and reinforced steel weigh more. It's not a racing car.

Conversely, if it was a very poor market, the risk management in the portfolio should kick in and the worst anticipated decline would be -6 percent. So, if one year it does -2 percent, the portfolio isn't broken. This is important so that you know the reasonable range of expected outcomes and aren't blindsided by it when it happens.

People sometimes ask me why their portfolio did not keep up with the market. Curiously, they only ask this after the market has risen sharply (they never ask why we protected them when it went down).

If you want to have full market returns, then you have to take full market risk. For the U.S. stock market, that means if you want an average return of 10 percent, then you must be prepared for years when it goes down more than 40 percent. (Yes, this has happened. Several times.) And you must also be prepared for years when it goes up 55 percent. (Yes, this has happened. Once.)

Good drivers don't over-drive their cars. And good investors know how fast their portfolios can go on highways and how slowly they'll move in heavy traffic.

Keep Adequate Insurance

Most of the time, people focus on planning for things going right: the traffic will be light, the tires won't go flat and they'll get there on time. And most of the time, that's true. But it's also prudent to have a spare tire in the trunk, the insurance paid up and a flashlight in the glovebox.

The reality is you only have the luxury of planning for things going right after you've prepared for things going wrong.

Several years ago, I had the odd coincidence of meeting two clients who went through very similar tragedies, and had two very different outcomes. Sam and Kevin were both in their late thirties, each had two small children. And both were widowed within the past year. For one, his wife died of cancer. For the other, she perished in a car accident. Each was left with raising their children and rebuilding their lives.

Sam's late wife had significant life insurance coverage, both from her employer and from personal policies they had purchased years before. There was enough money to pay off the mortgage and provide a regular income, so he put his career on hold and devoted himself to raising his children.

Kevin's wife had only a small amount of coverage, about $50,000 from her group benefits plan. After funeral costs, paying some credit card bills and covering a few weeks off work, Kevin had almost nothing. At the exact time he wanted to be most available to his children, he had to work double shifts to cover his wife's lost income.

What was the difference between Sam and Kevin? Both loved their wives and cared desperately about their children. Both were educated and had nice homes and cars. It wasn't until disaster struck that the material and primary difference was that one had good insurance protection and the other didn't.

A proper risk management plan helps you ensure that misfortune doesn't turn into tragedy.

No Towing

Towing another car just doesn't work. Do not let anyone else hook their broken financial car to the back of yours. If they've crashed, or run out gas and need help, it's fine to assess the situation. But you are not a mechanic or a tow truck. You cannot repair their damage and you should not blow your resources or wreck your car to do so.

I've had several situations where a client enters a new relationship with someone who is not financially successful or savvy. This is an accident waiting to happen. Fortunately, each time it's happened, I've been able to see it coming and warn my client of the dangers ahead. Towing someone else slows you down, burns a lot of gas and can take you both into the ditch.

Last year, I nearly played matchmaker for two clients who were in a remarkably similar position. Both were doctors, both divorced and both tired of the dating scene. As they each had financial independence, they were very aware that some people would date them to win their wallet rather than to win their heart. By being cautious, and rightly so, they found it very difficult to start new relationships. When I heard each express the same concerns, we obtained their permission to make introductions. At last report, they have had some good conversations, but I don't think Cupid's arrow has struck. :(

Shit Happens – Deal with It

If you have a fender bender, you deal with the damage, repair the car and keep moving. You don't walk or take the bus.

You will have a losing investment and markets will not go your way all the time. Everything moves in cycles, and by now I've explained how to recognize and weather those cycles. Once you've gone through a few up and down markets, you'll know what they feel like too. Remember those feelings so you learn from them.

Markets don't crash. Only novice investors do, when they destroy their portfolios by being surprised by a completely normal 14 percent intra-year market correction.

Share the Driving

How you travel through life is more important than where you started and where you finish. It's not your final resting place that you should care about, it's the road you took, the experiences you had and the people you loved, and who loved you, along the way.

If you are blessed to have a partner to share your life, then let them drive some of the time. Visit their waypoints and experience how they drive. Both of you will be more engaged and happier during the trip.

You both need to know how to drive because at some point, each of you will have to. Through death, disability or divorce, each person needs to know how to manage the family's financial affairs. One of the greatest gifts you can give your spouse is the ability to manage their money with dignity and independence. If you love them, do not leave them helpless and stranded. Teach them how to drive and give them the confidence of being behind the wheel. Both of you should attend the annual planning and review meetings. Both of you should know your professional advisors and be comfortable with the relationship.

10

Final Signpost

You Can Lose a Lot of Money Chasing the Last Nickel

This has been one of the greatest pieces of advice, after Stein's Law, I've ever received. (Stein's Law says: If something cannot go on forever, it will stop.) As an investor, I've learned that it is far better to be early, and leave a bit of money on the table than to be late and see losses accumulate.

Bulls can make money, bears can make money, but pigs and chickens get slaughtered.

If you have a winning investment, then be sensible about banking some profits as it goes up. Taking some chips off the table when fortune smiles on you is a good idea.

This idea also applies to spending money. Whether it's paying for great professional advice, buying a car or taking a vacation, the difference in quality at the margins can be huge. I've stayed in three-star hotels and I've stayed in five-star hotels. Yes, they both have rooms, a TV and a shower. But wow, are the beds ever different. If you can afford it, there are times when spending just that little bit extra can make for a meaningful difference. Don't be thrifty all of the time. Life isn't fun if you're cheap.

Life is a paradox.

It appears before us, in our hopes and dreams, as a straight line leading us forward. We make our plans and route the most direct path to get there.

Yet, when we look back upon our lives so far, we can see that it has been anything but a straight road.

The road of life twists, bends and winds upon itself. It is a series of intersections and roundabouts; of turns made and not made; some right, some left. Sometimes by our choice, sometimes chosen for us. Sometimes with passengers, sometimes alone. Times we've run out of gas or been lost and needed help. And times we've had to figure it out on our own.

We've had destinations in mind and things we'd like to see along the way. And surprises. Always surprises.

One thing is certain: it's the only road we have.

You cannot be a passenger in your own life.

Life is also not a race. How you travel matters.

All of us need to know how to drive. It is your personal responsibility for understanding money and how it affects you. It's is not the government's problem and it's not your company's responsibility. It is not your friend's, your spouse's or your children's problem. It's yours.

If you feel you're not where you should be, then stop and figure out how to get back on track. Refocus and recalculate. Get moving and keep driving.

Your journey IS your destination. Grab the wheel and floor it!

See you on the road....

FAQs

What happens if my spouse and I have different opinions on retirement?

This is normal. It's called *marriage*. You probably have different opinions on lots of things, from your favourite toothpaste, how to stack a dishwasher or how to change TV channels. The key to solving all of these challenges is to *talk to each other* and *compromise*. The best approach to retirement is through interdependence. Find things you like to do alone and things you like to do together. Accept that you are a couple and unique individuals at the same time. And that love conquers all.

On our wedding day, my father gave Sue and me wonderful advice. He said, "In times of happiness, turn to each other and say, 'I'm grateful you're here'. And in times of trouble, also remember to turn to each other and say, 'I'm grateful you're here.'" Remember that and you'll be fine.

Can't I plan for retirement all by myself? Do I really need a professional advisor?

Most of financial planning and investing is common sense and discipline. Just like staying healthy is just eating less and working out. And if you're like me and the vast majority of people, this is very easy to say, and extremely hard to do. A great advisor is a teacher, a mentor and – most importantly – a coach. Every Olympian, every professional athlete has a coach. Shouldn't you?

How will I know when I have enough money to retire?

Use the 7-Step Retirement Income Planning model from chapter five to help you run the math. This will give you a good idea of how much you'll need and how much you'll need to save.

An even better idea is to engage with an accredited and experienced certified financial planner to run these calculations with you annually. Everyone's situation is different, complicated and involves many trade-offs and compromises. Also, retirement is not a straight line: what you spend one year may not be the same the next year. A personal and tailored plan is really the key.

How do I find a great advisor?

Get referrals from friends who already have one. See who's on TV and in the press. Check their credentials, their registration and history. Once you have a short-list of at least three experienced and qualified individuals, interview them. If they're good, they'll also be interviewing you during the meeting. Great advisors do not need new clients. They're not selling. Rather, they want to take on new clients whom they believe they can help.

During the meeting, ask about their philosophy and their process. If they have a team, who are they and what does everyone do? What experience do they have in working with someone like you? How would they define success in your case?

It's also important to ask yourself if you would be a good client. Are you coachable? Are your expectations reasonable? What is it you want out of the relationship with an advisor?

I don't want to invest in mutual funds.

This is a common refrain from people who bought when they were greedy and sold when they were scared. Let's be clear: a mutual fund is simply the box the investment comes in. If you bought a bond mutual fund, it's simply a professionally managed and diversified portfolio of bonds. If you bought an equity mutual fund, it's a professionally managed and diversified portfolio of stocks. Saying that mutual funds are the problem is like blaming dirty clothes on a box of Tide. It's not the thing, it's how you used it.

There are legitimate pros and cons to every investment technique and product. Used properly, mutual funds can be an excellent and ideal investment tool for many investors. Like anything else, paying attention to what it is supposed to do, what it isn't supposed to do, who's running it and what it costs are all important considerations to make before investing.

I think stocks are too risky. What do I do?

There are a lot of ways that people will define risk. My favourite (and also Warren Buffett's) is that "risk is not knowing what you are doing". This applies to investing as well as gas barbecues, scuba diving and dancing in public. Owning stocks means you are owning a business. Consider the companies you deal with daily. If you drink Coke, would you think Coca-Cola is a risky business to own? If you drive a Mustang, would you think owning Ford is risky? How about where you bank, the computer you use or the company that owns the mall where you shop?

The record is that investing in the world's best companies is the most effective, most reliable and most consistent way to create wealth. It beats gold, it beats real estate, it beats diamonds and it certainly beats bonds and T-bills.

Again, the issue is never the investment. It's what you *do* with the investment that matters. Buy great companies and enjoy the dividends. That's how you become a great investor. Easy to say, hard to do. That's why almost all investors need a coach to keep them on track.

Acknowledgements

My wealth management practice is built around a team of outstanding professionals. When I say, "me", I usually mean, "them".

Similarly, it took a team to help me write this book.

This book has lived in my head for many years. I must thank my coach and friend Chris Flett for helping bring it out into the open. Chris, thank you for your advice, guidance and leadership. Not only did we get the job done – we had a great time doing it. And yes, I'm already working on the next book. ☺

I want to thank my amazing family at Raymond James who have been actively looking after clients and finding a way to carve out the many hours needed for me to write. I'm very fortunate to have Pedro Ostia-Vega, Andrea Thompson and Nik Zabaljac on my team. They keep my promises. You guys are awesome and I appreciate your professionalism, dedication and unconditional support.

Finally, I'd like to thank my wife, Sue and children, David & Olivia. I am so very grateful for the love, support and joy you bring into my life every day. You are always my inspiration and I have built all of my dreams around you.

About the Author

Darren Coleman started in the financial services industry in 1992 and with Raymond James in 2012, providing comprehensive wealth services for a variety of clients. During this time, he has been managing brokerage offices, spearheading industry trends and leading his team at Coleman Wealth to new territory.

Among Darren's many professional accreditations are Canadian investment manager, financial management and fellow of the Canadian Securities Institute, with a Level II life insurance license and an honours bachelor of commerce from Ryerson University. He was one of the first Canadian professionals to attain the professional financial planner, certified financial planner and certified hedge fund specialist designations. Due to his success as an advisor in alternative investments, he was the first advisor to sit on committees for the Alternative Investment Management Association (AIMA), and on the board for the Hedge Fund Association, as a member and instructor.

Darren is also licensed in both Canada and the United States as a portfolio manager and a financial advisor. In this capacity, he has a unique ability to assist investors who have money and family on both sides of the border and find themselves caught in the space between two very different legal, tax, investment and compliance regimes.

An industry veteran before coming to Raymond James, Darren held management and advisor positions at major bank-owned brokerage and financial services firms. Through this experience, together with his involvement with industry boards, he has built a network of professional relationships with the industry's top managers, firms and executives, through which he is able to offer his clients superior due diligence, access and insight.

Darren is part of Raymond James' Canadian flagship branch in Toronto and he is considered a champion of their cross-border service offering. He frequently speaks at conferences and educational events and currently sits on the editorial board for Advisor's Edge Report for Canadian investment professionals. He can also be seen as a recurring panel member on "BNN Advisor", a show produced by the Business News Network (www.bnn.ca/advisor) and dedicated to supporting advisors on handling their most pressing issues; the place where the pros turn for help.

Darren also donates his time to serve on the investment committee of the Community Foundation of Mississauga and participated as one of the 'stars' in their "2016 Dancing with the Mississauga Stars" competition.

To book Darren to speak at your conference or event, or to order custom orders and bulk copies of this book, please email: coleman.wealth@raymondjames.ca or call 1-877-363-1024.

www.ingramcontent.com/pod-product-compliance
Lightning Source LLC
Chambersburg PA
CBHW071947110426
42744CB00030B/630